# The Rose
## and the
# Thorn

# About the Editors

**Don Mullan** is a bestselling author from Derry whose first investigative book, *Eyewitness Bloody Sunday* (1997), was officially recognised as a primary catalyst for the Bloody Sunday Inquiry that led to British Prime Minister David Cameron's historic apology in June 2010. He is the author/editor of several books including: *A Glimmer of Light* (Concern Worldwide, 1995); *The Dublin and Monaghan Bombings* (2000); *A Gift of Roses* (2001); *The Little Book of Francis of Assisi* (2001); *The Little Book of Archbishop Oscar Romero* (2002); *The Prophesy of Robert Louis Stevenson: Damien of Molokai – The Leper Saint* (2009); *The Narrative of Frederick Douglass - An American Slave* (2011); and his boyhood memoir *The Boy Who Wanted to Fly* (2010). He is currently working on a worldwide Pelé legacy project; a World War I initiative in Flanders, commemorating the 1914 Christmas Truce; and, in partnership with the acclaimed sculptor Andrew Edwards, is developing a number of public works to celebrate the themes of Sport for Development and Peace and inspirational human rights leaders such as the ex-slave and founder of the Civil Rights Movement in America, Frederick Douglass.

**Audrey Healy** is an author and freelance journalist whose work has been published in, for example, *Ireland on Sunday, Sunday Independent, Longford News* and *Roscommon Champion*. A native of Rooskey, County Roscommon, she is the author of five books: *St Thérèse in Ireland, Dubliners: What's the Story?, Contacted* (co-written with Don Mullan), *The Singer and the Song* and *Mick Flavin – Celebrating 20 Years*.

# The Rose
## and the
# Thorn

☙

Reflections by Irish people
on their recent
highs and lows

Compiled by
Audrey Healy and Don Mullan
Foreword: Aine Lawlor

Published by
a little book company
11 Hillsbrook Crescent
Perrystown
Dublin 12
Ireland
Tel/Fax: +353 1 455 5453
e-mail: albc@eircom.net
www: alittlebookcompany.com

ISBN 978-1-906077-09-9

Book design and artwork: Glen Powell
Produced in Ireland by Betaprint Services

*Don:*

## **To Kristin Leary**

*An Irish-American friend whose energy, intelligence and grace have been an invaluable support in pursuit of a project aimed at finding common cause between the great diasporas of Ireland and Africa in America.*

*Audrey:*

## **For Sharon, with love**

*'A circle is round it has no end, that's how long I want to be your friend!'*

– Anonymous

# Contents

## *Foreword*

The best questions are often the simplest. That question Barbara Walters asked Barack Obama – What was your rose and what was your thorn? – struck me as a brilliant question. The kind of question that would make a person think a little before they answered.

Since Don Mullan got in touch with me to tell me about this book, I've thought a bit about that image of the rose and the thorn and why it works so well, not just for Barbara Walters and Barack Obama, but for all of those who have so thoughtfully contributed to this book.

What's clear when you start reading these accounts is that for so many of us the rose is those we

1

love and happy times spent with them. The thorn is so often illness, loss and loneliness. It is striking how often the same pattern is repeated in the lives of so many different people.

The rose is the most popular flower in the world. It is the symbol of love. Its velvety petals are like a baby's skin. Its scent is intoxication. The rose is the essence of long, balmy, summer days. We are living well when we have days where we really do wake up and smell the roses.

But its thorns are vicious, and always a surprise, snagging you as you reach in to touch the flower. Some of them are small, bristly things that break off under your skin to irritate for hours; some are huge, curved weapons that dig deep and draw blood.

With one comes the other. As the rose and the thorn are one, so are love and loss. Again and again in this book it is the love of friends and family that provides the rosiest moments. And missing those we love, the thorniest.

Over this past year, the weather and nature have been uncannily in tune with the economic crisis. The International Monetary Fund came to Ireland and the weather hit the deep freeze. In my garden I watched the bare branches of my roses, nothing but thorns. The very idea of their summer blowsiness, the pinks and blushes, creams and reds and purples seemed incredible. But now they're throwing out new leaves. Glossy, bronzy new foliage that promises the roses, the flowers I most love, within a few months.

Poets often associate the rose with fleeting pleasures to be savoured. We all know the expression 'gather ye rosebuds while ye may', but the rest of Robert Herrick's verse puts it more clearly:

Gather ye rosebuds while ye may,
Old Time is still a-flying;
And this same flower that blooms today,
Tomorrow will be dying.

We can't hold back winter, and no one who has written for this book has been able to avoid life's thorns completely. But there is always summer, and even in a bad Irish one the roses can be relied on to cheer us all up.

And the same cheer can be found in the serious, the rueful, the joyful and all the rest of the roses and the thorns described in the following pages.

It is nice to know that a short item in a busy *Morning Ireland* programme had the impact to inspire Don Mullan to make this come about, with the support of his colleague Audrey Healy. And I'm glad that the proceeds are going to the Irish Epilepsy Association.

Read and enjoy.

**Aine Lawlor**
**RTÉ** *Morning Ireland*
**March 2011**

# Introduction

The thorn from the bush one has planted,
nourished and pruned pricks more deeply
and draws more blood. – Maya Angelou

ABC's Charlie Gibson and George Stephanopoulos
first aired the story of the Obama family's dinner-
time tradition of 'roses and thorns' on 24 February
2009. They had just shared a White House lunch
with the newly elected President Obama, who had
given them an insight into what the family talk about
when they relax together over their evening meal.
Stephanopoulos explained:

They go around the table and everyone's supposed to talk about one rose – one great thing that happened that day – and one thorn – a bad thing that happened that day. And at one point, I guess it was after a particularly difficult day here at the White House, it must have been an especially difficult one, Malia said to her father, 'You've got a really thorny job.'

Seventeen months later, on 29 July 2010, President Obama appeared on ABC's popular women's chat show *The View*. This event caused a stir, not only in the United States, but worldwide, as it was the first time that a sitting US President had paid a visit to a daytime talk show. RTÉ Radio 1's *Morning Ireland* covered the occasion.

During the interview, Barbara Walters, one of America's most respected broadcasters, raised the Obama family tradition, 'We understand you sit at night with your wife and your daughters and you do "the rose and the thorn" right? You still do it?'

'We still do it,' replied the President, 'although Malia's at camp and Sasha's at a friend's house, so it's just me and Michelle.'

Then Walters asked, 'In the last month what has been the rose and what has been the thorn?'

## INTRODUCTION

'In the last month the rose has to be a couple of days we took in Maine with Michelle, Sasha and Malia,' he answered. 'We went on bike rides and hikes. You know the girls are getting old enough now where – they're not quite teenagers yet, so they still like you.' The audience laughed. 'But they're full of opinions and ideas and observations and it's just a great age,' he continued. 'Malia just turned twelve and Sasha's just turned nine, and it couldn't have been a better couple of days.'

When asked about the thorn, the President drew more laughter when he answered with his own question, 'Where do I begin?' Then he thoughtfully responded:

> . . . the country has gone through a tough stretch. Since I took office when I was sworn in – I know you showed the inauguration – we were losing 750,000 jobs per month, the economy was shrinking at a pace of about 6.5 per cent, which is unheard of since the Great Depression. So the last twenty months has been a non-stop effort to restart the economy, to stabilise the financial system, to make sure we are creating jobs again instead of losing them and in the midst of all that we've also

had the oil spill [in the Gulf of Mexico]; we've also had two wars; we've also had a pandemic, H1N1, that we had to manage, and a whole host of other issues.

What has been gratifying is the fact that the economy is beginning to stabilise and grow again; and what has been satisfying is seeing how resilient the American people are. As much as you said it's been tough for me, the truth is, it's not tough for me . . . think of what the American people have gone through: losing jobs, seeing their home values going down, their 401Ks declining. You know, those are the folks I draw inspiration from because I get letters every night from them and I read them and as tough as it's been, they remain hopeful and they remain optimistic about America and so I don't spend a lot of time worrying about me, I spend a lot of time worrying about them.

Walters pressed him further: 'One thorn, the biggest thorn this past month?'

Well, you know, the reason it's hard to answer is the things the media may focus on

are not necessarily the things I focus on. I have to sign letters to parents of children who have been killed in Afghanistan, or the husbands or wives of people who have been killed in battle. And that gives you a sense of perspective that is different from what is going on in cable-TV on any given day.

At the end of the *Morning Ireland* segment on the interview, presenter Aine Lawlor commented, 'Isn't that a wonderful question, "What is your rose and your thorn?"'. And then the programme moved on to other matters. I, however, pondered Aine's remark and concluded that yes, it was a wonderful question. I waited until after 9 o'clock before calling my friend Audrey Healy in Longford to say, 'Audrey, I've got a good idea for a book.'

Within a week Audrey and I were sitting in the coffee shop at Eason's bookstore in O'Connell Street, Dublin, and mapping out the steps necessary to bring this book to fruition.

Having drawn up a list of people in Ireland and abroad we would approach, we sent letters or emails about the Obama family tradition and the Barbara Walters question. Without offering direction, we asked each contributor to respond to the rose and

thorn question as they pleased based on their experience in the past year. Some correspondence went unanswered. The majority of people we approached were extremely courteous and we thank all contributors who are published in this our first volume.

The result is a moving volume of reflections that offer a fascinating insight into the personal and social concerns that dominated the thoughts of Irish people in the recent past.

The rose and thorn analogy is, indeed, a simple but clever way to draw forth reflections of both an individual and global nature. In our back garden in Dublin we have three rose bushes, all of which can be appreciated close up or from a distance. Up close I can breathe deep the joyous fragrance of each individual rose and sometimes prick a thumb or finger in the process. Or, from the perspective of my attic window, I can look down and enjoy a festival of delicate intertwining soft white, yellow or pink petals crowning each stem, jealously guarded by jagged sentinels who demand respect and care. Later in the book I have written from both perspectives about two 'rose and thorn' experiences of my own.

I'm particularly happy to know that royalties from the book will be donated to Brainwave – The

Irish Epilepsy Association. Epilepsy is a condition that my colleague Audrey Healy has coped with following the removal of a brain tumour when she was a teenager. Like so many people with the condition, Audrey strives to live her life to the fullest.

Audrey and I hope that this will be the first of a series of such books in Ireland and I am also happy to be working with American journalist Megan Specia on a US edition.

In the year that Ireland will, by happy coincidence, welcome the source of the idea behind this book, President Barack and Mrs Michelle Obama, Audrey and I can offer no better advice than the following German proverb:

> Instead of complaining that the rose bush is full of thorns, be happy that the thorn bush has roses.

**Don Mullan**
**April 2011**

## Brainwave's Mike Glynn

### THE THORN

My job is Chief Executive of Brainwave – The Irish
Epilepsy Association, but at the moment I am also
the elected President of the International Bureau for
Epilepsy (IBE), which is the international body
representing all organisations for people with epilepsy
around the world. 2010 started out with thorns all
over it for Brainwave. The Health Service Executive
(HSE) announced major cuts in our funding, and
this at a time when our public fundraising was in
severe difficulty. It meant that everyone employed by
Brainwave had to take a cut in pay, but at least we did
not have to let anyone go. Our great staff were thus
able to continue to provide the best service possible

for those people with epilepsy and for the parents of children with epilepsy all around Ireland. One significant development in the year was the HSE's appointment of a clinical lead in epilepsy, the first time it has properly recognised the condition.

## THE ROSE

The biggest rose in my year was the achievement of the first European Epilepsy Day, held on St Valentine's Day, with major events all around Europe and at European Union level. St Valentine has been the patron saint of epilepsy for many hundreds of years. This day highlights epilepsy as a public health issue for the first time right across Europe. Politicians and members of the public are made aware of the problems people with epilepsy face and what actions and research need to happen to improve their situation.

## *Former Taoiseach Bertie Ahern*

Bertie Ahern is from Dublin and first ran for election in 1977. He was elected sixth leader of Fianna Fáil in 1994 and became the youngest ever Taoiseach in 1997. He resigned as Taoiseach and leader of Fianna Fáil in 2008 and did not contest the 2011 general election.

THE ROSE

The highlight of last year, for me, was my beloved daughter Cecelia's marriage to David Keoghan.

THE THORN

The low was the death of my two great friends Rory Brady (former Attorney General) and Ciaran O'Driscoll.

## *Television Presenter Claire Byrne*

Claire Byrne co-hosts RTÉ's *The Daily Show* with Dáithí O Sé. The programme covers topics from human interest to celebrity gossip, political intrigue to sporting success, and international events to national preoccupations.

### THE ROSE

I completed two half-marathons last year and, despite the hard training and the injuries, the sense of personal achievement was my rose. I never thought that I could run further than a couple of miles, but I soon began to believe that I could do more than I ever thought possible. Most of the obstacles were in my head and when I crossed the finish line I felt like a world champion! I am now

preparing for my third and, who knows, maybe the marathon might be my goal for this year.

THE THORN

My thorn was the devastating news that someone very young and very close to me had been diagnosed with incurable cancer. Her strength and endurance in the face of extreme adversity has been inspiring, but all of us who love her (and she herself) know that there will not be a happy ending. It puts everything else into perspective.

## *Sports Commentator Brian Carthy*

Brian Carthy is from County Roscommon and is the Gaelic games correspondent/commentator on RTÉ Radio 1.

THE ROSE

Thursday 30 December 2010 is a date etched in my mind. On that joyous day, in the tranquil setting of St Malachy's Church, Ballymacilroy in County Tyrone, the stunningly beautiful and radiant Michaela, with her husband John McAreavey by her side, told me it was the 'happiest, happiest' day of her life.

Just a short time earlier, we had witnessed her proud dad, Mickey Harte, walk his precious daughter up the aisle to the place where John was eagerly waiting to greet his wife-to-be. Michaela had often

spoken to me about how lucky she was to have met a person of the quality of John, who shared the values that were so characteristic of her own life.

Michaela was so full of joy. She could not stop smiling. We all remember her beaming with happiness beside her dad when he guided Tyrone to All-Ireland Senior successes in 2003, 2005 and 2008. But the happiness she most assuredly showed on those occasions does not even remotely come close to the joy and delight on her face on the day she married the 'light of her life', John.

After the marriage ceremony, Michaela, John and guests visited Mickey's home place, next door to the church, for some refreshments before travelling to the wedding reception in the Slieve Russell Hotel in Ballyconnell, County Cavan. Michaela wanted to spend some time with her uncle Paddy, who had made a special effort to walk to the church for the nuptials, despite struggling with ill health. The time Michaela and John spent with Paddy and the rest of the family was precious. Sadly, Paddy passed away some weeks later.

Michaela was very close to all her family. She had a special relationship with her mother, Marian. At the wedding reception, Michaela said she wanted John and herself to have the same happy marriage as

her 'Mummy and Daddy'. Michaela also adored her brothers, Mark, Michael and Matthew. But there is no doubt that she had an exceptionally close bond with her father. She enjoyed the fact that she was known as 'Daddy's girl'.

Michaela was Mickey's most loyal supporter. She loved football and was a totally committed follower of Tyrone. Michaela was only seven years old when her dad took over as manager of the Tyrone Minors in 1991 and she never missed a single championship match from that time on. She was always by Mickey's side on big-match days, dressed in the latest fashion with the white and red of Tyrone featuring strongly.

Michaela was an ambassador for Tyrone football. She helped out at training and had the rosary beads out during games in which Tyrone were involved. She had great regard for all the players, none more than Peter Canavan, Brian Dooher, Stephen O'Neill and Seán Cavanagh. The players in turn had total respect for Michaela. She was still very young when Paul McGirr died while playing for Tyrone Minors in 1997. She also had to cope with the death of Cormac McAnallen in 2004. Those shockingly sad deaths brought her even closer to her dad and helped strengthen her faith and form her own unique character.

Michaela was the first person Mickey wanted to talk to when Tyrone won the All-Ireland Senior Championship for the first time in September 2003. I was on the sideline for RTÉ Radio and all of us reporters and journalists had to wait several minutes before Mickey would do any interviews. Mickey and Michaela had to speak to each other first. I can still recall the moment the beaming Michaela came through the crowd to embrace her dad. It was a once-in-a-lifetime moment.

Michaela wrote a note in September 1997, after Tyrone lost to Laois in the All-Ireland Minor Final, stating that Tyrone would win the Minor title in 1998, the Under-21 crown in 2000 and the Senior title in 2003. She confided this in me in early summer 2003, by which time two of the aims had already come to pass. Michaela then promised to be a guest on my radio programme on the evening of the final if Tyrone emerged victorious. And who was I to doubt her total faith in her dad and in the Tyrone team? True to her word, Michaela and Mickey came up to level seven of the Hogan Stand for the post-match broadcast and she explained in her own gentle and sincere way about her predictions that had come to pass.

Brian Carthy

## THE THORN

Just eleven days after the 'happiest, happiest' day of her life, Michaela was taken from us in devastatingly cruel circumstances. I will never, ever be able to put out of my mind the sense of shock and utter disbelief I felt when I heard the news of Michaela's death on Monday afternoon, 10 January 2011. My wife and I were collecting our daughter from school when Mickey called to tell me the awful news that Michaela had died on her honeymoon in Mauritius. Shocked to the core, he was heartbroken and utterly devastated.

I visited the Harte family home later that evening to offer my condolences to Mickey, Marian, Mark, Michael, Matthew and the extended family. I felt helpless. Many of the wonderful people I had met at Michaela and John's wedding were there with tears in their eyes, sympathising with the family and lending support in any way possible. No one could come to terms with the tragedy.

Michaela represented everything that was positive and enriching in a human being. Words of mine are hopelessly inadequate to describe her extraordinary qualities. She had a strong faith and was a gifted schoolteacher. She was fiercely proud of her roots and was a fluent Irish speaker. But I will

remember Michaela for her sheer goodness, her gentleness, her loyalty, her good humour, her generosity and her smile. Since her untimely and tragic death, her smiling face has been shown on television screens all over the world. It was a humbling experience for me to be asked to bring one of the offertory gifts to the altar at Michaela's funeral mass.

In recent years Mickey has spoken to so many people who have suffered bereavement and have been left stricken with grief. His message has had a constant theme: if you wish to hold those people who are gone in high regard, think of what good you can find in them and bring it into your own life. Mickey and Michaela have provided solace and hope to so many people who encountered sadness in their lives.

The Hartes and the McAreaveys will need all the support possible now that their beautiful and radiant Michaela has gone – all too soon. But she has left a lasting legacy and her spirit will live on and provide comfort to all who mourn her passing. Truly, God was at his brilliant best the day Michaela was born.

Slán abhaile a Michaela dhíl. In iothlainn Dé go gcastar sinn.

*[Brian Carthy's full tribute to Michaela appeared in the* Irish News *on 14 January 2011.]*

## *Former Broadcaster and Political Adviser*
## *Una Claffey*

Una Claffey is a former political correspondent in RTÉ and was a political adviser to then Taoiseach Bertie Ahern.

THE ROSE

Late in the evening of 9 March last year my ship, *M/V Prince Albert 2*, pulled away from the harbour at Ushuaia, capital of Tierra del Fuego, at the southern tip of Argentina. We were bound for Antarctica. As we sailed down the famed Beagle Channel, glass of champagne in hand, I marvelled at the fact that I was actually making this journey and was about to cross the dreaded Drake Passage.

I still don't know precisely what prompted me to

visit this vast and virtually unknown part of the world. A sense of adventure was important. To walk in the White Continent, to experience the white silence, to see, first hand, the icebergs, to go where several brave, intrepid Irishmen had gone before me and where, even today, few make this extraordinary journey, were all motivating factors. I was not disappointed.

True, our excellent vessel made the expedition a far more comfortable one than the courageous men of Shackleton's *Endurance* experienced. Safety standards were rigorous and our transport by Zodiac inflatable to various landing points made the journey seem almost ordinary. But the thousands of penguins, the giant albatross nesting, the whales and seals, the many sea birds and the towering icebergs were evidence that this was no ordinary voyage.

Two particular moments gave me great pride. Appropriately, I first stepped onto the White Continent at Almirante Brown Point. Founder of the Argentine Navy, William Brown was in fact born in County Mayo. How wonderful that this was where I was to experience my first footfall in Antarctica! My emotions were matched only by those I felt at Grytviken. This is where Shackleton, the great Irishman who explored this inhospitable but thrilling part of the world, is buried. A former Norwegian

whaling station, it also carries a memorial to the magnificent Kerryman Tom Crean, who accompanied Shackleton on his explorations. I was reminded yet again that, small island though we may be, we have made our contribution to the world.

## THE THORN

At a small reception in 2007 given by Taoiseach Bertie Ahern to mark the departure from government service of the Attorney General and myself, I remember saying there was no one with whom I would sooner ride into the sunset than Rory Brady. I can still see Rory, head thrown back, laughing heartily. As I stood at his graveside, just three years later, his laughter still echoed.

Rory died tragically, leaving behind his beautiful wife, Siobhan, and two lovely daughters, Maeve and Aoife. Hours before he got a chance to return fully to his practice at the Bar he was struck by a deadly illness. Almost to the very end I believed he would survive. Our telephone chats were full of optimism, and determination on his part, as he explained the details of his condition before going on to discuss the latest political events. He desperately wanted to live.

Ten years older than Rory, I met him through my work with the then Taoiseach. Maybe it was our mutual pride in being Dubs that cemented our friendship. Certainly from my perspective, his generosity, intelligence and commitment to public service marked him out as a colleague of rare distinction.

Rory loved life. He took pride in the fact that at one point he had worked for the same law firm in Chicago as Barack and Michelle Obama. He loved to travel. He revelled in his connection with Harvard University. During his years as Attorney General he worked tirelessly in the service of his beloved Republic. His public profile was low. That was how he wanted it. But anyone who encountered him professionally was impressed by his knowledge and understanding of the Law and its application. It will be for history to recognise his role in the Peace Process.

Last year saw many tragedies in Ireland. The tragic death of Rory Brady was one of the more significant.

## *Aid Worker Sharon Commins*

Sharon Commins was working as an aid worker when she was kidnapped, along with her colleague Hilda Kawuki, in Sudan's war-torn region of Darfur in July 2009. They were held in captivity for 107 days. Now based in Dublin, she continues to work in the aid sector.


THE ROSE


On 1 February last year my niece sprung into this world, bringing with her a magic that melted away the remaining remnant of our family's ordeal. Equipped with an innate curiosity, baby Kate has brought out the best in everyone and transformed the house into a place of pure happiness. Having her on the scene has underlined for us the fact that what

really matters in life are the people you love and their relationships. The rest takes care of itself.

## THE THORN

I feared that the memories of the cold nights spent wondering if this Irish girl would ever escape those mountains were frozen inside me. You cannot delete sadness, and I had times when I felt destroyed. The beautiful side of it is how you then get pushed on by life forces: and that's survival.

So many ordinary Irish people, even ones I don't know, wanted to tell me their own personal suffering of deeply troubling events that beset their lives. They wanted to demonstrate by example that I too could weather my storm. Such simple acts of innate decency and humanity had a profound effect on me and helped me to make sense of it all. I am rejuvenated to realise that suffering need not destroy, that it also throws up equally powerful aspects of joy, empowerment and calmness.

## *Businessman Louis Copeland*

World-renowned as a master tailor and provider of men's designer suits, Louis Copeland's company has evolved significantly over the last hundred years. The name Louis Copeland & Sons is now synonymous with men's tailored clothing and high-end fashion in Dublin.

### THE THORN

Well, I think the thorn has to be the downturn in business. Sometimes you go along and you have a bad day but then you see somebody in worse circumstances than yourself and you give yourself a kick in the ass and say, 'Right I'm in great form,' then you get a great day . . . then the next day, you go and visit someone in hospital and it makes you realise how lucky you are and you're alright again.

I have to say that I think in two years' time, when we look back on this period, we will say that the recession was probably the best thing that ever happened to our younger people because they assumed the good times were how it was all the time – but it isn't like that.

THE ROSE

I'm sixty-one years old and have three grandchildren. They are the 'up' in my life – watching them grow up. I know it is a cliché, but I am probably spending more time with them than I did with my own children.

Also, I have been working in the business, with my father before me, since I was ten years of age and I describe business as a bit like a game of snakes and ladders. Up to 2007 we climbed up towards the very top of the ladder and then in 2008 we fell right down to the bottom – and now we are back on the first rung again. So it's a bit like getting back to where you started. It is actually enjoyable because you have to call on your resources and you know where the pitfalls are.

## *Broadcaster Pat Coyle*

Pat Coyle is a national broadcaster and journalist. Originally from Derry's Bogside, she now lives in Dublin with her teenage son and daughter, Paul Óg and Sadhbh.

## THE THORN

The fallout from the horror of clerical child sexual abuse and its cover up, as revealed by the Dublin Archdiocese report: abusive priests protected by their superiors and prioritised over their victims to protect the Church's good name; duplicity, and the use of theological niceties and codes of canon law to defend the indefensible and dispense a bizarre form of clerical 'justice'; and the completely inadequate response to the survivors in the wake of the report from the Church both in Rome and at home, with a few exceptions. This was the Church I was part of, and not just on the fringes. I was right in there, singing my heart out every Sunday with the Star of the Sea Choir.

I really wanted the survivors of clerical abuse to know how appalled I was at what had happened to them. That it truly mattered to me and that as a Catholic still in the Church I would listen to them and respond positively to what they were asking of the institution that had inflicted such unspeakable harm on them and their families. I believe most practising Catholics wanted that too. But there was no collective way for us to let the Church know that ('it's not a democracy' they often remind us) or to demonstrate publicly our solidarity with the survivors. Even worse, Mass attendance was being used by some as a barometer of comforting conformity: 'All is fine; the faithful are still going to Mass.'

The familiar powerlessness I've felt as a woman in the face of the clerical Church (and have for a long time been inured to) returned with gut-churning force. One thing I knew, but couldn't articulate very well, was that my singing days were over for the foreseeable future. And lest I became a statistic for a good news press release about Mass attendance, I made the decision to abstain from something that is at the core of my faith. Although fellow choir members responded kindly and with understanding when I told them my decision, I felt alone and so alienated from the institutional Church that I wondered whether I was a Catholic at all. 'They so don't get it,' I thought. 'Or maybe it's me.' And then I got a phone call that introduced me to the rose.

## THE ROSE

Sr Carmel Clarke is a contemplative Carmelite nun in an enclosed order in Glenvale, Newry, County Down. She spends her days praying and making altar breads and righting grievous wrongs. She has rung me to ask a favour twice in twenty years. The first time was to help a mother found guilty of embezzlement that Carmel knew was innocent. My then husband and I were working as journalists for the BBC in Northern Ireland and she wanted us to investigate the case and prove the woman's innocence ahead of her appeal. We did and she succeeded.

This time Carmel was looking for me to write a cover endorsement for a book of poem-prayers by a friend of hers, Michael Maginn, Parish Priest in

Lurgan, County Armagh. I agreed to do it because it was Carmel asking, but in truth I was really worried that his work would be a schmaltzy mess of soppy poems and saccharine prayers. I was wrong. Below is the first poem I read (reproduced with kind permission of the publisher: Carmelite Publications, Glenvale, Newry).

### Bereft of Song.

(For those who continue to minister faithfully)

*By the rivers of Babylon*
*there we sat and wept remembering Sion.*
*For it was there that they asked us,*
*our captors for songs,*
*our oppressors for joy.*
*Sing to us they said, one of Sion's songs.*
*How could we sing the Lord's song on alien soil?*
*(Psalm 136)*

The ballad of biblical exiles
touches a raw contemporary nerve.
During their long sojourn in the land of Babylon,
The captives are taunted for songs.
Bereft,
broken-hearted,
they could not bear to sing their songs of home.

## PAT COYLE

What cause for song today?
Litanies of abuse explode around us
Like improvised mines beneath our feet.
Hearts ripped out,
lives torn apart,
once solid ground opens to swallow us whole.
If we dare to sing at all
In this beleaguered landscape,
we should sing quietly,
so as not to disturb,
or offend,
or attract undue attention.

*Lord,*
*better maybe not to sing at all,*
*in case the word goes out*
*that those who sing today,*
*are the churchy equivalent*
*of the loathsome holocaust denier.*

Strong stuff. The words of a priest who 'got it' and
was prepared to call it. Some day, I'll sing again.

## *Broadcaster John Creedon*

Cork native John Creedon presents a mix of contemporary Irish and international tracks to take the listener on a melodic journey into the evening on RTÉ Radio 1.

THE ROSE

The rose is the birth of my granddaughter, Mollie. That was a particularly wonderful moment because we lost our first granddaughter, Lucy. My mother was one of ten girls! Mollie is an absolute star and we wouldn't take it for granted. After what happened with Lucy, I'm aware that pride comes before a fall and we have something to be proud of and something to be grateful for and I'm amazed at her teeny-weeny fingerprints and her little face . . . she's remarkable

. . . she's amazing. She's as bright as a button. Thank God. She's so pretty. And at the moment she's sleeping ten or twelve hours and even that is said with pride! Gratitude and awe!

## THE THORN

The thorn of last year would have to be my friend Gerry Ryan's sad passing. I knew and worked with him during the 1980s and 1990s. I would never claim to have been his bosom pal but I had been close enough to him on a professional level and we grew to know each other on a personal level as well. He was a great character who went on to become a great pal. We worked together and even sang together!

The thing about Gerry really is that he genuinely was a great broadcaster and he had a great relationship with the public. He was absolutely huge and I suppose we thought that he would keep going forever. If somebody had told me that one of our greatest broadcasters was going to go, I wouldn't have believed it would be Gerry – so it was a huge shock. He was a great family man as well. We went on a lot of foreign trips together, did a lot of gigs on the road and enjoyed many funny times and he was always a very attentive dad, so his children are the

people who obviously were the closest to him. Although there was an incredible public outpouring of grief at the time of his passing, the grieving really was for his family who knew him best and 'knew the scent of his skin'. They are the ones who are really going to miss him.

It makes you think – there's always that kind of sobering thought for those of us hitting our middle years – who's next? When? How?

You never know when your time will be up.

Gerry's death really wasn't in the script at all.

I suppose the moral of the story here is that there's a connection between the two: the highs and the lows, birth and death. The truth is – and it's my own personal belief – death is not the opposite to life, death is the opposite to death and whatever energy keeps going round and round, that energy is universal and applies to those who went before us and those who will come after us.

Death is not the end.

## *Matthew Cummins*

Matthew Cummins lives in Dublin with his wife, Susan, and teenage daughter, Holly. He is awaiting a heart transplant.

THE ROSE

My rose is to wake each day. To see my wife's eyes, green, peaceful and inspiring. To see my teenage daughter blossom, like a bud on the stem of the rose bush. A teenager full of the joys the world has to offer. In the uncertain situation that I find myself in, where I require a heart from another soul, each day has precious moments.

I have a new relationship though. My wife doesn't mind because she gets to see me. My new relationship is a mechanical one: a surgical device

that is to bridge me towards a heart transplant. The insertion of this device has taken away my pulse, but that doesn't mean I am not alive.

To see life grow, from people to plants, through the seasons is like a beautiful rose. To walk amongst the flowers and to smell the air is a gift from heaven. No other person could have helped me through the procedure better than my wife and daughter. As each day passed, I grew stronger. Their smiles injected me with the willingness to get better, faster. I knew their smiles brought pain to them. Knowing I will have to go through surgery once again is very daunting, but that is how it is. Their smiles inspire me. The kindness of man warms me. Often I pray for a day that will enable me to leave this device behind and continue to watch my rose and bud flourish. To continue to walk the dog, say hello to others, but mostly to see and hold my rose.

THE THORN

My thorn is the device I must be connected to, to live. Without it I wouldn't see my rose. It is at times a love/hate relationship, but my machine doesn't talk back, it merely makes a subtle humming noise. At night the hum echoes loudly in my ears, a noise that

reminds me of what I went through over the past number of years. A noise so subtle, so delicate, yet I think: no noise, not good. The percutaneous lead that runs through my body is like a mechanical umbilical cord. It powers me. Yet it tethers my free spirit. It reins me in, sustains me. At times ages me. But it is a relationship that must be. No unconditional love. Literally, it is a thorn in my side.

Still I must wait, and hope to see the flower bloom.

## *Newscaster Bryan Dobson*

Bryan Dobson is a newscaster and journalist and one of the most recognised faces in Ireland. He is a presenter on RTÉ Television's *Six One News*.

### THE ROSE

My roses are my family and in particular our children, Sophie and Hannah. Each day they surprise and delight us, and throughout last year (as in other years) we celebrated their successes and encouraged them not to be downcast by setbacks. Sophie, who is completing an arts degree at University College Dublin and is an active member of the Musical Theatre Society, had her first part in a professional production, as one of the chorus in *Beauty and the*

*Beast* at the National Concert Hall. Hannah, who has studied ballet for many years, danced in a show staged by her performance school and, for the first time, was on points. These were definitely rosy moments for us.

## THE THORN

The big thorn is what has happened to Ireland and how our children's future has been stolen by a combination of greed, incompetence and stupidity.

On a more personal note, last year the death occurred of my friend, the photographer Bill Doyle. Although Bill was in his mid-eighties, he never acted his age and rarely seemed old. I had known him for almost thirty years. He was a great artist and a great companion, and I shall miss him. Bill was one of a 'great generation' of Irish men and woman who endured tough times, and in his case helped to forge a national identity of which we could be proud. He loved Ireland, its landscape and its people. May he and his kind be an inspiration as we set out to rebuild our country.

## *Actress Roma Downey*

Derry-born Roma Downey resides in Malibu, California with her husband, Mark Burnett, and their children. She performed with the Abbey Players on Broadway and achieved international fame as the leading lady in the Emmy Award winning series *A Woman Named Jackie*. She later starred as the angel Monica in the CBS hit *Touched by an Angel*.

## THE THORN

This past year I turned fifty. Wow! It brought with it some 'fear of letting go'. From fear, I saw the glass as half empty.

THE ROSE

Then the big day came and went and I found that I 'let go' of fear. From there, I saw the glass as half full. Same situation, different attitude. My thorn became my rose.

## Broadcaster Joe Duffy

Joe Duffy is one of Ireland's most popular broadcasters. From Monday to Friday each week he presents *Liveline* on RTÉ Radio 1.

### THE ROSE

The highlight was the commencement in October last year of the building of the long-awaited cystic fibrosis unit for adults in St Vincent's Hospital in Dublin. Long overdue, this unit – with basic, individual, en suite rooms – is urgent and necessary. It had been buried and delayed by the Celtic Tiger and hospital politics.

JOE DUFFY

THE THORN

Apart from the daily immiseration of the nation propelled by the unending stream of bad economic news generated by criminal Irish male bankers, the moments of deep joy and pain are intensely personal. My lowlight of last year was the sudden and tragic death on Friday 30 April 2010 of Gerry Ryan. The nation lost a great broadcaster, entertainer, listener, therapist, comedian . . . his friends lost a loyal, wise adviser and confidant and his family lost a great father, husband and friend.

### *Broadcaster Myles Dungan*

Myles Dungan presents the weekly *History Show* on RTÉ
Radio 1, where guests explore events ranging from medieval
times to the recent past.

## THE ROSE

It was a year in which my youngest, Ross, graduated
and my eldest, Amber, got engaged. Enough good
news for anyone in one year really. The former event
took place, entirely through the medium of Latin, in
the baroque surroundings of the Examinations Hall
in Trinity College, Dublin. The less salubrious, but
still joyful, location for the latter was under an
umbrella on Dalkey beach. I attended the conferring
but wasn't invited to the proposal. Odd, that.

The two middlers, Rory and Lara, had good years too. He won an award for best short film producer at the Celtic Film Festival and she got a scholarship (the last ever?) to start a science PhD in Trinity. My cup ranneth over.

Thanks to the wonders of house-swapping, my wife and I managed to make a relatively inexpensive return to old haunts in Berkeley, California for a solid month in June. It wasn't quite the same as the six months we spent there in 2007, but at least we didn't feel like tourists. We were able to visit old friends and then go home every night to a house full of wonderful books and the NBA Championships live on the telly. Bliss, that.

Professionally, I got the best present from RTÉ that a boy could ever ask for – and I had been for a while – my very own history show on the radio. And it wasn't even Christmas. Now it is every week. I'm a bit worried about what someone once said in *Henry IV Part I*: if all the world were sporting holidays to play would be as tedious as to work – or something like that anyway. Hasn't happened yet. Cool, that.

THE THORN

The biggest thorn was a mood rather than a particular

event. It was one of sadness, watching Ireland become the new sick man of Europe. The fact that we are not alone in the intensive care ward is of very little consolation. I remember back in 1988 when Northern Ireland was going through the Gibraltar, Corporals and Michael Stone killings and I was in the United States making a radio documentary. I watched it all from afar with a sense of rising horror and powerlessness. It wasn't as if I would have been able to do anything if I'd been at home, but I felt denied of context. I wondered if there would be anything left when I got back. This time it is much the same, except I'm right in the middle of it, overwhelmed by context. I often feel – like a lot of people I suspect – that I'd love to just ignore it all for a few weeks and listen to Lyric FM. But, as someone who is expected to present current affairs programmes on radio, I don't have that particular luxury.

I know I'm in the privileged position of having a good job. I'm not one of the 430,000 unemployed people studying their options and perhaps contemplating life somewhere else entirely. I don't have any solutions to offer. I wish I had. But I know one thing: if it ever looks like the madness of the early 2000s is starting up again, then I'll be the grumpy, toothless, old spoilsport in the corner going,

'I wouldn't do that if I were you. You weren't around in 2002 were you?' I might even change my name to Cassandra and try and force articles on the *Irish Times* and documentaries on RTÉ Radio on the history of the Great Irish Recession 2008–2???.

## *Sculptor Andrew Edwards*

Andrew Edwards is one of the UK's most distinguished sculptors. His paternal grandparents came from Cork and he currently lives and works in Stoke-on-Trent. His public monuments have been unveiled by, amongst others, Pelé, Archbishop Desmond Tutu and Princess Anne.

THE ROSE

My dad used to grow roses, so I can't help thinking of him when thinking of them. I also think of Antoine de Saint-Exupéry's *Little Prince* and what the rose in that story said about people: 'People? there are six or seven of them I believe, in existence. I caught sight of them years ago. But you never know where to find them. The wind blows them away.

They have no roots, which hampers them a good deal.'

Last year the wind blew me back to Cork, the ancestral home of my family. Well, of the people in the old photographs I inherited from my dad's side, but never met. My collection of old photos has led me to say over the years that my best friends are those I haven't yet met. The best part of my job as a sculptor of public and private commissions is the people it allows me to meet. In pursuit of sculpting a monument to Frederick Douglass, I have been delighted to see more and more of County Cork and some of the places in my old photographs. It has also let me meet delightful people there.

Like Saint-Exupéry, my father's dream was flying. He joined the Air Force just before the outbreak of World War II. I remember him telling me about the unexpected horrors he saw as a sixteen-year-old wireless operator and gunner who had lied about his age. When I walked out onto the icy November Cork airfield and saw the awaiting ATS 72, I felt the excitement of a sixteen-year-old. I had crossed the Irish Sea many times before, but this was my first time by propeller engine. It sounded different, it smelled different and I felt charmed and touched.

My flight had already been delayed by a few

hours because of heavy snow and a faulty engine so it was approaching midnight when we began our descent into Manchester. Most of England was at a standstill due to the severe weather and all London airports were closed. Just as I started to make out the yellow glow of the approaching runway lights, the plane snatched upwards and began climbing again. The pilot had previously announced that Manchester was under more fresh snow and he was circling in a holding position awaiting the airport's reopening. Three more times the engines changed pitch as our altitude dropped tantalisingly close to landing before sharply pulling up. After over two hours in the air for what should have been an eighty-minute flight the announcement came without a hint of irony, humour or sarcasm: 'The airport isn't clear for us to land. Liverpool, Birmingham and East Midlands are all full and we don't have enough fuel to hold for another hour, so we are going back to Cork.'

When eventually, the following day, we did manage to land in Manchester, I was happier than I can ever remember to finally make it home.

## THE THORN

I was in the room when the families of Brian Clough

and Peter Taylor met for the first time after twenty-three years. In fact, I was the reason for the reunion. I have been honoured with many prestigious public art commissions and I am equally proud of every one, but I have never felt such a weight of expectation and personal significance as I did when reuniting these two men in statuary. Two giants in the field of English soccer. Amongst many titles and trophies, they won back-to-back European Cups in football, a feat still unsurpassed, and they did it from unglamorous beginnings, with teams they took from lower divisions and players that had been overlooked or would likely have stayed undiscovered.

Clough and Taylor generated belief beyond measure and not just for the clubs, teams and players, but for the ordinary people they represented so well with cutting frankness and forthright honesty. They were generous and supportive within their community, taking direct measures to help families suffering poverty, despair and hardships during the years of power cuts, three-day working weeks, industrial disputes, redundancies and mass unemployment that marked the 1970s. I know this to be the case because I came to know their wonderful families during 2010 and they are of the same spirit: honourable, humble and sincere. With

the generous personal contribution of the Clough and Taylor families, the project to depict and honour these two great men and the qualities they represent became the largest and most ambitious sporting landmark monument in Britain: Unity Plaza at Pride Park, Derby . . . and I was the artist. Why then is this story a 'thorn'?

It is because the two friends, Clough and Taylor, 'muckas' that their wives Barbara and Lilian describe as 'the kind of friend you may be very lucky to meet one of in a whole lifetime', died without being reconciled and without seeing just how much they meant to others. They were so important to me as a boy because, in the first instance, they meant so much to my father. And there too is something else not reconciled. I never told Dad that he was my hero and will always be my inspiration.

I dreamt of Dad last night. First time for ages and the first time I think I ever saw his face in a dream. His hair was black like it was in a photograph from when I was aged two or three and we were on holiday. We weren't doing anything in the dream, we were just there together. Did it make me happy or sad? I'm not sure. I guess both. I was consoled, glad I had known him but I couldn't quite smile. But now I have written it down, I am smiling.

## *Broadcaster Larry Gogan*

Larry Gogan is a popular Irish DJ famed for his RTÉ 2FM radio show *The Golden Hour*, during which he plays old favourites and classic songs from yesteryear, as well as his classic 'Just a Minute Quiz'. He began his broadcasting career in the 1960s.


## THE ROSE

There's no doubt in my mind that the greatest moment of last year for me was the birth of my granddaughter Poppi, who was born to my son David and his wife, Niamh. Poppi is my tenth grandchild. Before her came David, Holly, Jodie, Nikki, Jorja, Noah, Jamie, Isaac and Ben.

I always remember when my first child, Gerard,

was born. What a joy it was to see this living being that I had created. To watch a child grow from a tiny mite and to see him or her going through all the stages to adulthood has to be the greatest gift that one can get. My late wife, Florrie, and I were blessed with four more: Orla, David, Grainne and Sinead. Each one of them special, each one unique, with their own personality and talents.

When you marry they say 'may you see your children and your children's children'. It is truly the greatest gift of life and I can only hope that the world they grow up in will be a happy one – full of peace and kindness.

## THE THORN

Thankfully I didn't have a personal thorn last year, but the thorn that has blighted our country has to be the way we had to give up our sovereignty and how we have to depend on the International Monetary Fund and the European Union to keep Ireland going. I come from a family who fought for Irish independence. My father, although only a boy, fought in 1916 and most of his cousins were also involved. What those men would think of having to more or less hand over our country to foreigners, I

shudder to think. It's a terrible legacy we're leaving our children and grandchildren, who'll be paying this back for generations.

How it happened has a lot to do with greed. People wanted more than the next person: a bigger car, a more stylish kitchen, etc. If you hadn't got the money, you didn't worry, you borrowed it – the banks would give you all you wanted. What a terrible price we have to pay for it all now. To me, that's the greatest thorn to hit every man, woman and child in this country.

## *Singer-Songwriter Kieran Goss*

Kieran Goss was born and raised in County Down. His albums include *Brand New Star*, *Worse than Pride*, *Red-Letter Day*, *Out of My Head . . . The Best of Kieran Goss*, *Blue Sky Sunrise*, *Kieran Goss Trio Live* and *I'll Be Seeing You*.

## THE ROSE

My rose was a trip to Nova Scotia. I have only recently started working in Canada and I was amazed when, during our show at a festival in Canso, Nova Scotia, I introduced the song 'All That You Ask Me' and then the crowd gave a huge cheer! I started singing the song and when I got to the first chorus, the whole crowd sang along. It was a magic moment. I had no idea how they knew it. There we were in Nova Scotia for the first time and two thousand people were singing my song. I was physically on the stage but my mind went straight back to the day I wrote the song in the kitchen of my parents' house in Mayobridge, County Down. It really struck me that my songs have a life of their own and can travel much further and faster than I can. It was wonderful.

Talking to people after the show, I found out that Archie Fisher has been singing the song as the final song of his concert for the last ten years in Canada and that one of Canada's folk music legends, Garnet Rogers, sings the song at his shows too.

## THE THORN

The thorn was the death of Gary Gillen. Gary was our lighting engineer and, more importantly, our great friend for more than fifteen years. Along with Vinnie Higgins on sound (Vincenté y Geraldo!), we toured the length and breadth of Ireland together and came to rely on Gary to, in his own words, 'turn any fuckin' toilet into a real gig!'

Gary was an artist and a perfectionist and he would often stay behind long after the sound check because he wanted everything to look just right. He cared about what he did and he cared about people. We will miss his warmth, his hilarious, sarcastic sense of humour, his friendship, his company and his love. The world is a lesser place without him in it.

## *Singer-Songwriter Mick Hanly*

Limerick native Mick Hanly joined forces with the cream of Irish traditional musicians in the late 1970s to record *A Kiss in the Morning Early*. He later took a lead role in the group Moving Hearts and his best-known song is 'Past the Point of Rescue'.


THE ROSE


For the last three years I have been working in SOS Kilkenny. SOS stands for Special Occupation Scheme. It works with people with intellectual disabilities and their families in Kilkenny and its environs. Every week I oversee a couple of hourly musical sessions with different groups. My aim is to get the participants to entertain themselves with whatever musical turn they can contribute, and generally we manage to have enough performers to fill the hour. I provide some guitar accompaniment and some help with choruses. The fact that I've recorded a dozen albums and written a chart-topping US country hit cuts little ice at these gatherings, and if I can't play the chords to 'Mamma Mia' or 'It's a Long Way to Tipperary', then I might as well pack my bags and go home.

One of the outstanding performers in the group is Raymond Lyng. Raymond has a beautiful light voice, a superb ability to hold tuning and an excellent sense of time. He also has a wonderful memory for lyrics and a vast repertoire. Last year he sang in an SOS concert to a packed and partisan audience at the Watergate Theatre, Kilkenny. Raymond did two songs and I provided the accompaniment. He brought the house down with his renditions of 'The Fields of Athenry' and a Johnny McEvoy song about Michael Collins, which I think is called 'The Big Fella'.

In the audience was one of the SOS staff members and her nine-year-old son. The following day she told me that as Raymond and I took our bow, her son turned to her and said, 'The fellow on the guitar is very good; what's wrong with HIM?'

## THE THORN

In the scale of thorn damage, the following is but the snagging of a thread, but then my pleasures are simple. Here on the Station Road in Thomastown, our house backs onto a couple of open fields that roll down to the banks of the Nore. I realise that the patch we inhabit is only on loan from Mother Nature for a limited period and that, in time, she will reclaim it and allow the savage diversity to thrive untroubled by lawn feed and bug-bottle. We have a rickety wooden fence, which the wildlife, apart from a few cattle, refuse to recognise, and so they come and go at will, leaving their scratchings and turds where they please. It is not unusual to find Caesar the dog, sniffing at a rolled-up hedgehog, or to hear him go mental because a fox has decided to take a stroll within spitting distance of the fence. It doesn't end there. Every bird, from goldfinch to wagtail, is a daily visitor, and every year there are a dozen varieties of nest in the shrubbery.

And joy of joys, we have nesting swallows. From St Patrick's Day onward, I look forward to their imminent arrival. Some years ago they commandeered a shelf in my tool shed, and had been playing happy families there since. I love their chatter and their swooping, and do my best not to get in their way. They go about their business repairing the previous year's nest, and usually manage a couple of clutches. In 2010 they came, did some DIY on the nest for a few days and then quit. One day they were busy adding new mud, next day they were gone. I was sure that they would return and bless the summer with their acrobatics and twittering. They didn't. Why? Did they get the sniff of the collapsed property market and decamp to Scotland? Where would they find a safer place than my shed: it being inaccessible to all human beings apart from myself? Why, with the good vibes of 2009's successes (two clutches of five) still lingering, would they choose somewhere else? I pray that it's a one-off. Fingers crossed for this year.

## Singer-Songwriter Mike Hanrahan

Mike Hanrahan is from County Clare and worked with Stockton's Wing, Finbar Furey and the late Ronnie Drew before embarking on a change of direction to pursue a career in cooking with Darina Allen at Ballymaloe Organic Farm.

## THE ROSE

The rose in my life is my music. It has always been central in my life and when it blooms I know true happiness. My parents, brothers and sisters grew together with the sound of music permeating throughout the house. My brother Kieran and I have continued to support each other throughout our music careers and beyond. There is a special bond between us and the

occasional gigs are always a joy. Creatively, music has given me the canvas to express my personal reaction to events and people who influence my life. I have been lucky in music to get to travel, meet wonderful people and then take to the stage to sing my songs. Although I recently left the industry, I still play the odd gig, a few sessions and practice regularly to keep myself tuned in.

## THE THORN

It is ironic that the thorn in my life is best described in a song I wrote called 'The Garden of Roses'. The song was, and still is, a personal response to the harrowing stories from the victims of clerical abuse. The State, the Church and Society failed so many of our innocent children who were sexually abused and then condemned to a life of psychological trauma. Painful and powerful testimonies finally brought the reality to our daily lives and it is Ireland's shame that its so-called pillars of society were allowed to create and get away with such human destruction for such a very long time.

The Garden of Roses

In the garden of roses
Where you came by

## MIKE HANRAHAN

Beautiful roses
The eyes of a child
In your secret desire
You cut it all down
Now petals lay scattered
On tainted ground
In the garden of roses
Beautiful roses

How your temple has fallen
The walls cave in
We witness the sanctum
In their evil sin
But a river once frozen
Deep in the mind
Flows on like a river should
In the eyes of a child
In a garden of roses
Beautiful roses

In the garden of roses
where you came by
In the garden of roses
Beautiful roses
In the garden of roses

## MIKE HANRAHAN

A river once frozen
Down deep in the mind
Flows on like a river should
In the eyes of a child
In the garden of roses
Beautiful roses
In the garden of roses
Beautiful roses.

## *Newstalk's Garrett Harte*

Garrett Harte is Programming Director of Newstalk 106–108, Ireland's independent national talk radio station. He was involved in the launch of the station in 2002 and produced the drivetime show *The Right Hook*. He is a Donegal native and married to Nicky. They have two children, Maisie and Joe.

THE ROSE

The rose is my darling mother, Rosalie, who celebrated her eightieth birthday on 6 November 2010. Married for fifty-seven years, still rearing nine children, not to mention twenty-four grandchildren and countless school-friends, Mammy is the boss in the extended Harte family. Her youthful perspective

and optimistic outlook on life enrich the lives of all who have the delight of being in her company. A proud Irishwoman, her acute political antennae would ensure her election to political office today. However, she chose a different route to channel her passionate political views and married a good-looking butcher from Lifford, who went on to become a TD!

I also have the pleasure of sharing birthdays with Mammy as she brought me into this world on 6 November 1970. To celebrate the two landmark birthdays in 2010, the extended Harte family, forty-three members in total including siblings, in-laws and grandchildren, plus toys and Facebook, all descended on the Great Northern Hotel in Bundoran for a family weekend away. Friday night was my fortieth celebrations and involved a themed 1970s night, with wigs, flared trousers, dodgy music and more wigs. Saturday was the 'rose' night as we went back in time to the 1930s. It was a special evening of huge love for Mammy/Granny. The highlight of the evening was listening to a tenor sing a melody of my parents' favourite songs and seeing in their eyes the fond memories of their long life together and indeed sharing a tear for all those who are no longer with us. And one simple wish: to go back in time for just a minute and relive those fond times again.

Our great family weekend was also shared with the annual Bundoran Elvis Festival. To see ten Elvis lookalikes tucking into their full Irish breakfast is a sight to behold, but there is only room for one rock 'n' roll star in the Harte house: Rosalie.

## THE THORN

It was with deep sadness that I watched Ireland brought to its knees – I watched as friends and family were forced to leave my country, leave their home, leave their communities, uproot their children, and seek a new start. The majority of those who have left have thankfully found new employment and are content in their new life. Of course, they miss their family and friends. The tragedy is that we have lost them, lost their influence on society, their enterprise, their energy, their social spirit and their patriotism. It is vital that those of us lucky enough to have a job and to remain in the country redouble our efforts to rebuild this great nation, engrain a new sense of pride in our people and ensure that we create a society that is more just, more honourable and where integrity is practised as well as preached.

## *Author Audrey Healy*

Audrey Healy, co-editor of this collection, is an author and freelance journalist from Rooskey, County Roscommon.

## THE ROSE

My rose of last year is energetic, fun loving and always has a smile on his face. He sprang into this world weighing seven pounds and eleven ounces on 27 August 2010 at 9.04 p.m. He has brought inexpressible sunshine and joy into my life and that of his parents, his three older sisters and his grandparents. My rose is my much-loved new nephew and my Godchild, Matthew Gerard. Apparently the name Matthew means 'a gift from God' and when I

look at the newest addition to our family, I know he was a gift worth waiting for.

## THE THORN

My thorn of last year was witnessing, and indeed sharing – along with my friends and colleagues, the pain of the current economic climate. The majority of my friends are journalists and I quietly observed from the sidelines as one by one they all took pay cuts, and some went on to subsequently lose their jobs. Our cosy circle of friends dwindled a little as some had to leave the area and go further afield in search of more secure employment.

Readers who know the town of Longford will be aware that the past year has seen the demise of two familiar landmarks. Founded in 1936 by Vincent Gill, the *Longford News* was a stepping stone for many of Ireland's talented journalists and offered valuable work experience for both writers and photographers. I and fellow ex-employees of the newspaper gathered on a sunny day last summer to bid it farewell as it ceased production. It was a sad day when it closed its doors for the final time.

Yet the biggest catastrophe to hit Longford last year was the tragic fire that engulfed the town's pride

and joy, St Mel's Cathedral, leaving a building in ruins and a community in tears. Memories of that time still evoke feelings of shock and disbelief on many faces. The extraordinary thing about that Christmas Day inferno and its aftermath was that it didn't really matter who you spoke to – any creed or nationality, any age, whether or not they had been baptised, confirmed or married in the Cathedral, or even those who don't believe – they all felt a sense of loss and a deep grá for the building that stood so majestically and proud in our town.

Today that much-revered building is still derelict inside and it is expected to take up to five years to restore it to its natural beauty, but this is where the rose blooms again. The goodwill of the parishioners who have lost their place of worship has been extraordinary and they are doing all they can to help ensure that that five-year goal is achieved. Amidst the grieving for the Cathedral, there is now hope in the form of the chiming of bells once again.

There is no doubt that with the determination of the clergy and the enthusiasm of the people, St Mel's will reign again.

## *Author Michelle Jackson*

Michelle Jackson is an Irish author. Her novels include *One Kiss in Havana*, *Two Days in Biarritz* and *Three Nights in New York* and she is co-writer of a non-fiction book *What Women Know*.


THE ROSE

The rose is easy: my friend Catherine, with whom I closely shared the precious teenage years, returned to live in Dublin last summer. She had lived abroad since we graduated from university twenty-three years earlier. We met in secondary school aged thirteen and over the years have seen each other through all amounts of joy and heartache. Wherever Catherine chose to live, I visited her – and I can trace the pattern

of both our lives as we wove those visits with important events such as new jobs, marriages, childbirths and sadly deaths. When we both turned that pivotal age of forty we shared a weekend together in the seaside town of Biarritz in southwest France. While there, we concocted the plot for my first novel. Neither of us could have imagined how much both our lives would change from then. Every rose has its thorn and for Catherine it was the sudden loss of her husband at the young age of forty-two. But now, two years later, she is picking up the pieces and, with her beautiful daughter – who is only a year older than my own – in tow, she has come back to live in Dublin. I am looking forward to all the new memories that we will be making and sharing together with our daughters.

THE THORN

The thorn is more difficult to write about as there are so many layers to the issue that bother me. I fear for the women of the world and the harsh cruelties and traditions that they have to suffer and endure. An example of this is the story of the Nigerian woman who has been seeking asylum in Ireland. Her dilemma has drawn many different reactions from

people. For me, I think the focus should be on the issue of female genital mutilation (FGM) that she is trying to protect her daughters from and asylum should be granted until her daughters are safe to return to Nigeria. It saddens me greatly that my country will not protect her and in doing so highlight the need for governments in the European Union and other Western societies to condemn this practice and demand that the nations concerned – predominantly in Africa but also in Asia and the Middle East – no longer allow FGM to continue.

FGM is an example of the oppression of women and the defacement of their femininity that is gaining momentum all around the world. The covering up of their faces with scarves or burqas is another way of controlling women. Although I am a deeply spiritual person who has huge belief in God, I do not believe that religion has helped the world to progress. Under Islam and the Catholic Church there is a horrible attitude to sex and women that will and can only be corrected when women accept and acknowledge their inner strength and turn their backs on these patriarchal institutions.

But the rose in this thorn is hope and I have great faith in the beauty and strength that women possess – we are after all the creators of life in our wombs

and this is the greatest human achievement possible. My friend Dr Juliet Bressan and I have gathered stories, wisdom and advice from women all over the world and compiled a book – called simply *What Women Know* – because we deeply believe that women can rectify these situations if they turn to each other and support each other and maybe then the balance of the sexes will be equal or shared hand-in-hand at least.

## *Solicitor Gerald Kean*

Cork-born Gerald Kean is a well-known solicitor based in Dublin. He set up his practice, Keans Solicitors, over fifteen years ago and has represented a number of prominent people from the entertainment industry.

THE ROSE

This is not meant to be in any specific order of preference! The time I spend with Lisa, my fiancée, and Kirsten, my daughter.

I am a very happy and positive person. I enjoy and live each day to the full. I have a great love of a nice cigar, red wine, good food, Manchester United and meeting people. I also look on the bright side of everything. Even when diagnosed with diabetes I felt

it was going to help me improve my fitness level and eating habits. This has proven to be correct. One must be positive.

Having spent time supporting and helping various charities I do feel it keeps one's perspective properly focused. The greatest smiles I saw in Cork last year were the parents of special needs children in Scoil Triest. They approach life with a wonderfully positive attitude. There are so many people with real obstacles in life and others should learn to appreciate their own good luck and fortune. I often feel we should turn more towards the strength and positivity of those people who face much more difficult obstacles in life and who cope with them in an extraordinary fashion. There is a great sense of self-satisfaction and achievement in helping others, spending quality time with family and friends and enjoying a variety of experiences in life.

## THE THORN

The loss of some great people: Paul Monks, Stephen Gately, Gerry Ryan, Mary Carmody and many other super people and friends. All of these individuals and others were simply too young to die. I still find it difficult to come to terms with the loss of my great

friend Patrick Rocca. I also find it sad to read on a daily basis about the loss of young lives on the roads and other tragic deaths. This is one thing I find difficult.

## *Actor David Kelly*

David Kelly is an acclaimed Irish actor, who has been in regular film and television work since the 1950s. He has appeared in *Fawlty Towers*, *Into the West* and *Charlie and the Chocolate Factory*.

## THE THORN

In 1937 a rose bush was planted in my front garden. It is there to this day. Now, at eighty-one years of age, I have begun to appreciate what a wonderful symbol it is. Down the years it has delivered immense pleasure as well as the not infrequent stab from the thorns. Last year's thorn was the near-fatal illness of my wife.

## THE ROSE

She is now fully recovered and that must be the main rose, but being blessed with a son and daughter of whom I am so proud and who are with me every day of my life, usually in person and when not, by phone, I realise that there are a lot of roses. Add to that a highly successful career doing what I love and a dog called Max and allowing for the few thorns that come with age, it doesn't have to be the rose season for me to enjoy rose after rose after rose.

## *Campaigner John Kelly*

John Kelly's brother, Michael, died on Bloody Sunday.
John was a tireless leader of the Bloody Sunday Justice
Campaign, which culminated with an official apology by
British Prime Minister David Cameron in June 2010. He
works at the Museum of Free Derry.


## THE THORN

I remember it well: Bloody Sunday, 30 January 1972.
Twenty-three years old. Brother of Michael, seventeen
years old. My younger brother.

His life was taken that day. Murdered by a British
paratrooper. What a waste of a young life. He was
lost to us. His future was lost to us. His loving, his
caring, his personality, his whole being lost to us.

What a shame. My family devastated.

My mother devastated. Never got over it. Lost her son. Lost forever. Never forgave. She died heartbroken. Sitting with him by her side in heaven. Happy now.

## THE ROSE

I remember it well: 15 June 2010. What a day. Nervous. Uptight. Emotional. Couldn't wait. Innocence declared. Michael vindicated. Everyone exonerated. Acknowledged to the world as being murdered. Unjustified. Unjustifiable. Wrong. Unbelievable outcome.

Families delighted. Derry delighted. The world delighted. Exhilaration everywhere. Smiling faces.

Paratroopers condemned. Murderers every one. Guilt laid at their feet. We were right. They were wrong. What a victory. Truth at last. Justice to be delivered.

We have overcome.

## *Sr Stanislaus Kennedy*

Sr Stanislaus Kennedy has written and published many books. She has also written thousands of articles that have been published in Ireland and elsewhere. She lectures on social issues and policies and is a frequent keynote speaker at many events.

THE ROSE

The rose of last year was being able to organise a national conference on mindfulness. The first annual 'Art of Being Still' conference, held in Dublin Castle, brought teaching and practice of mindfulness into the lives of many, many people, and continues to have a huge ripple effect right across the country.

## THE THORN

The thorn of last year would have to be all the financial cuts felt by the poor and vulnerable. The effects of this recession have pierced to the core those most in need – the low-paid people and those depending on social welfare – causing so much suffering and pain. Every day people are losing their jobs, their homes and at times their families because of the financial changes and uncertainties that they face. The people who never benefited from the Celtic Tiger are the ones suffering the most. That is a huge injustice.

## *Trócaire's Justin Kilcullen*

Justin Kilcullen is Director of Trócaire, the official overseas development agency of the Catholic Church in Ireland. Trócaire was set up by the Irish Catholic Bishops in 1973 to express concern for the suffering of the world's poorest and most oppressed people.

## THE ROSE

Gaza was very much in the news last year. This peaked around the incident of the flotilla carrying humanitarian aid to Gaza which was stopped by the Israeli Navy at the end of May. Nine people died and many more were wounded in a clash between Israeli forces and those on the ships.

Just one week later I arrived in Gaza on a visit that

had been planned for some time. I travelled through the territory with members of the Palestinian Centre for Human Rights, meeting with families and communities and hearing about how the aid blockade is affecting their lives. I was brought to meet an elderly man living alone in a substantial house surrounded by a small farm, just 450 meters from the Israeli border. His name was Mohamed Shurab, a retired construction engineer who had worked for many years in the Gulf States. He was reasonably well off and had put his four children through college. He had a tragic story to tell of the shooting dead of his two sons by Israeli forces. We listened, moved by his experience and the passion in his voice. He then brought us on a tour of his small farm.

This to me was a revelation – it was a mini-paradise. The ancient promised land of the Bible was described as a land of milk and honey, and here it was! He had a herd of goats, an olive grove and an orchard with oranges, dates and other fruits. He had beehives and delighted in removing pieces of the honeycomb for us, which we ate with relish. There were small irrigation channels carrying fresh water to his fields and making a pleasant gurgling sound. Since his sons were killed it was this farm that had kept him going. The place was delightful. However, a short distance

away loomed a watchtower on the Israeli border. Mohamed's peace is broken from time to time as the soldiers, out of boredom, take potshots at his house. He showed us eleven bullet holes in the wall facing the frontier. But he remains dignified and defiant. In a land laid waste by war and poverty, Mohamed and his farm stand out like a bright red rose amidst the rubble.

## THE THORN

Last year will be remembered as a year of economic crisis. It affected us all. My son was made redundant, but he is young enough to move to new experiences abroad that will stand to him in the future, hopefully at home. Meanwhile, I was cast in the role of having to make people redundant. No more than many others I never thought it would come to this. I had to face my responsibilities for the future good of Trócaire. The funds donated so generously by the public are to assist those in greatest need in the developing world. Our commitment to that mandate, as funds inevitably decreased, meant that jobs in Ireland would have to go. This has been the most difficult thing I have faced in my years in Trócaire. Those impacted were disappointed, shocked, angry and tearful. I felt all those feelings myself as I delivered the bad news. Never again, I hope.

## *Singer and Priest Liam Lawton*

Liam Lawton has successfully combined his love of music with his pastoral work. He was commissioned by Trócaire to write a music piece commemorating the 150th anniversary of An Gorta Mór (1845–49) and has performed in the White House and St Patrick's Cathedral, New York.

## THE THORN

Looking around the world and within Ireland one could write about many thorns last year, but I would like to write about something more personal. In the summer I lost the last of my surviving uncles in my father's family. John was just ninety years old and had lived a simple but very happy life. His passing marked the end of an era for me and for my siblings.

He had lived his life in a beautiful scenic corner of east Cork not far from the seashore, where as children coming down for summer holidays we longed for our first glimpse of the Atlantic Ocean from the top window of the farmhouse. John represented everything that is good about 'Irishness'. He had a great healthy respect for the land, for neighbours and friends and for faith and family.

The God I often heard him converse with was also found in the break of day when John rose to collect the cattle, in the birthing in the clay, in the changing seasons and in the breaking of bread on Sunday morning in the local church of Ballymacoda. In his ninety years John saw many changes in his rural neighbourhood, but adapted to all with great wisdom and insight. His love of Gaelic games never left him as he followed the feats of Cork in hurling and football, and especially of his local club. John's death was as natural as his birth, returning to his family and the God who created him. But his passing has left a great loss in our lives as we mourn not just this good man but also the values that he stood for and believed in. Perhaps the tears shed are also shed for an Ireland that is losing its soul, forgetting the values and virtues that the generations before us held and lived. Perhaps with all our cynicism we have

failed to see the real truth in the words of Peig Sayers: 'ní bheidh ár leithéid aríst ann'.

## THE ROSE

The old familiar saying that we should 'count all our blessings' is certainly becoming more realistic in the world we now live in. In considering the many blessings I received last year there is one that brought much joy.

My nephew was born eight years ago. A beautiful blue-eyed, fair-haired little boy, his smile would touch any heart. Not long after he was born his mother noticed that she could not hear him cry, as any normal child would, when hungry or in need of attention. Thus began a whole series of examinations, tests and eventually serious surgery. This little boy had a narrowing of his windpipe and had to undergo an emergency tracheotomy, depending on a tube that was to be his lifeline for almost two years. Over the years that followed he had seventeen surgeries. I marvelled at the expertise of his consultant Mr John Russell, whose skilful hands brought new life and hope into this vulnerable child and who continues to do the same every day in Our Lady's Hospital for Sick Children in Crumlin, Dublin. One night in the

hospital I heard a gentle voice singing a beautiful lullaby in another language. When I walked in I saw a young Filipino nurse with my nephew in his arms as he lulled him to sleep. I wondered if the little boy he held would ever speak or sing himself.

But every day small blessings become great ones. Every act of kindness, no matter how small, becomes an opportunity for hope and healing. In this place of great vulnerability, the light of each new day makes room for miracles. The many days and nights have grown into years and the tiny little boy has grown to take his place in our world. Last year he stood before his community to read at the local vigil Mass. He spoke loud and clear and prayed for those less fortunate. His family rejoiced in this miracle. His name is Daniel: the one who enters the lion's den and is unharmed.

## *Singer Jerry Lynch*

Jerry Lynch hails from Kilfenora, County Clare, where his family has had strong connections with the Kilfenora Ceili Band for generations. He is best known for his recording of 'A Silent Night (Christmas 1914)' by Cormac Mac Connell, now one of the most requested songs on Irish radio at Christmas time.

The rescue of the Chilean miners and the yoke of debt that has been placed on the shoulders of the Irish taxpayer for generations to come would be my rose and my thorn on a global scale. For the purpose of this exercise, however, I would like to make two personal contributions.

## THE THORN

Around the first week of September 2010, my wife and I were driving from Clare to Cork and were on the new bypass under the Shannon. We went through the tunnel and were driving in the right-hand lane behind some other cars on what is clearly a dual carriageway/motorway. A short while after emerging from the tunnel I noticed that an oncoming lorry driver on the other side of the carriageway was continuously flashing his lights and I wondered what was the reason. The car in front of us pulled over into the left-hand lane and I continued to overtake. Then the reason became very clear. We could not believe what was in front of our eyes. There was a car coming towards us in our lane against the flow of traffic. The driver seemed oblivious to his/her error and must have assumed that I was overtaking dangerously on a normal road with traffic flowing in both directions. I impulsively swung the car to the left and thankfully got out of the way. Luckily there was no car parallel to us, because I had no time to check. If there had been, I dread to think of the result.

I could use this example as the rose in that there was no accident, but in this case I want to use it as the thorn.

## THE ROSE

World Peace Day takes place on 21 September. To mark the event in 2010 the Instruments of Peace Centre on Dublin's North Circular Road organised an event at The Space in The Helix. It was loosely themed on the seasons and war/peace, and consisted of contributions from clergy, singers and musicians from different backgrounds and religious persuasions. I was asked to take part by Rosemarie Lucero, one of the directors of the Peace Centre, because she was familiar with a song I had recorded by Cormac Mac Connell, 'A Silent Night Christmas 1914'. It is about the Christmas Truce in World War I. The idea for the event developed out of the enthusiastic response of the students from the Loreto Secondary School, Balbriggan, County Dublin and the Lourdes Youth Choir, Drogheda, County Louth when approached by Rosemarie to join in making an effort to do something with a peace theme. They drew up a Peace Manifesto, which we all signed on the night, and are lining up a number of letterboxes through which it will be dropped in the future.

This is my rose. A group of students and their teachers from two different towns had the motivation and interest to spend their time (rehearsing) and money (each girl bought her own dress so that they would look the same) for no reward other than to be a part of an event about a desire for peace. When I think of the number of young people facing unemployment, a drug and alcohol culture, abuse, and the mess of a country they are inheriting, the enthusiasm and optimism shown by these young people gives me great hope for the future.

## *Broadcaster Alf McCarty*

Alf McCarty presents 'one of the best known music shows on [RTÉ] Radio 1 for the last two decades', *Late Date*. Each programme offers listeners the perfect blend of music and good company.

THE ROSE

The best age to be in your life is three!!! When I was three everything happened to me: I had my tonsils out, went to visit my auntie in England, kissed a girl – yeah that's right, Alfie kissed a girl . . . aged three. It would be another fifteen years before I had the courage to repeat that action, but when you are three you have no inhibitions. The reason I mention it is that last year my grandson turned three.

Connor Davin Poole, force of nature, spent all of last year in the three zone. Early in the year when he called my name, it came out as 'War WAARRR'; by the end of the year it came out as 'Granddad'. I kinda miss 'War Waarrr'. But there have been compensations. He and I like to play pirates, I threaten to 'AARRRharr tickle 'em with me fish fingers' and he likes to tie me up. Both of us are very happy. He has also developed the knack of telling me jokes, which he makes up on the spot. The main ingredients for these jokes are vegetables and bodily functions.

'Hey Granddad, why did the banana do his wees?'

'I don't know Connor, why did the banana do his wees?'

'BECAUSE HE WAS BURSTING!!!'

Or

'Why did the banana come down the chimney?'

'I don't know Connor, why did the banana come down the chimney?'

'TO STEAL THE PRESENTS!!!'

Stand-up comedian and philosopher, may he always have the ability to steal the presents. He asked my daughter recently, 'Mommy, are there any pirates?' She said, 'No, they're only in stories.' She didn't feel he was quite ready for Somalian pirate stories. He then wondered, 'Are there any dinosaurs?' When she told him that they are all dead, he responded, 'Just like John Lennon?' There is no answer to that.

He has now turned four and I say, 'BRING IT ON'.

## THE THORN

The news was simple. Yes, we have spotted something in the X-ray. You will need to meet with the consultant. No matter how you looked at it the result was the same: a cancer was present in the breast. The thoughts and emotions were spontaneous. Could it be wrong? Did they make a mistake? Why me?

We met with the consultant, who outlined the situation. The area affected was small, there would have to be a surgical procedure carried out and radiation therapy was a given, chemotherapy may also be involved. The fact that my late mother-in-law had had a mastectomy added further fears.

The operation went well, but another procedure

was necessary to take a further sliver of tissue – to be certain that the cancer had been completely removed. Radiation therapy and the start of a five-year course of tablets began. The good news was that the cancer was small, diagnosed early and removed. There was no need for the chemo treatment. Last year we passed the first landmark X-ray and have been given the all clear.

It was because of the screening process run by BreastCheck, the Irish national screening programme, that my wife was diagnosed with breast cancer. The first thought is that every woman should, as regularly as possible, go and have a mammogram; as should every man go for a prostate test. The other thought is that, despite the crippling hand of bureaucracy and the financial cutbacks in the medical service, the frontline care, expertise and basic human kindness experienced by my wife and me were phenomenal. Many, many thanks.

## *Journalist Patsy McGarry*

A native of Ballaghaderreen, County Roscommon, Patsy
McGarry is the Religious Affairs Correspondent of the
*Irish Times*. He also writes occasionally on social issues for
the newspaper.


## THE THORN

Without a doubt the thorn was the press conference
in Government Buildings, Dublin, late on Sunday
21 November 2010. I was covering nights that
weekend on the news desk at the *Irish Times* and
went along to assist our political reporter colleagues.
There, then Taoiseach Brian Cowen and then Minister
for Finance Brian Lenihan announced that the
Government had formally applied for a multibillion-

euro rescue package from the European Union and the International Monetary Fund, which would result in external oversight of the Irish economy for four years. Questioned as to whether this would also mean a relinquishing of our economic sovereignty, Brian Cowen said, 'a small, open economy like Ireland did not have the luxury of taking decisions without reference to the wider world'. The previous Monday he had said Ireland was not making an application for EU or IMF funding as the country was already funded up to the middle of 2011.

It was unbelievable. Yet, as happens with momentous events, the atmosphere in the room was muted and calm, even routine. It was as if the significance of what had been announced had not sunk home with the journalists present, most of whom were far too busy getting down details to reflect on the magnitude for Ireland of what they had just heard.

It was one of those lowest of the low moments in recent Irish history. Indeed, I was a bit dazed myself. But beside me, Vincent Browne was not. He was at his apoplectic best and got stuck into Brian Cowen about his personal responsibility for the catastrophe in Irish public affairs. I was not aware he was being televised live by TV3 at the time, but saw a repeat later, with myself silent and stunned beside Vincent,

who was beside himself. Part of Vincent's intervention was also broadcast by RTÉ, which then, foolishly, cut away and went back to the studio.

Vincent Browne did the State some service that night and his intervention had something of a cathartic effect for many of us. He let off some of the steam of the nation. But I have to confess that I also felt a twinge of sympathy for Brian Cowen and Brian Lenihan. Even then it was apparent that the implications of what they had just announced would, politically, be grim for them too. What a way to be remembered by history.

THE ROSE

I would nominate two such 'moments' from last year. The first was a visit to Budapest in October. It is a stunningly beautiful city, with lovely people and a shocking history. Well worth a visit, and very reasonable.

The second was my train journey across Ireland on Christmas Eve. I was going home. I love Christmas in Ballaghaderreen but this journey home was very special. I got the train from Connolly to Boyle, where my brother Declan picked me up. The journey west was like something out of Narnia. The country was

covered in great depths of the whitest snow, with trees and hedges all along the way dangling great lengths of hoarfrost and snow. It was wonderful and I was held spellbound for the full journey. To see the green familiar transformed into something altogether otherworldly was a terrific Christmas present. It was, of course, another great Christmas in Ballagh, where the temperature on Christmas Day was minus 14°C. I had never experienced such cold, but hardly felt it as we did the Christmas rounds of family and friends' houses. It was a white Christmas to remember, it had to be the whitest Christmas I've ever seen.

## *Singer Charlie McGettigan*

Charlie McGettigan has worked with Maura O'Connell and Eleanor Shanley amongst others. He won the Eurovision Song Contest with Paul Harrington in 1994 and has since released *Rock 'n' Roll Kids*, *In Your Old Room*, *Family Matters* and *Stolen Moments*.


## THE THORN

People often said to me, 'Your father is a fine looking man.' I remember, even as a child, thinking what a handsome man he was. He always had his hair Bryl-creamed to the last and looked like the 1940s film icon Robert Taylor. He was always really well turned out, with carefully co-ordinated shirts, suits and ties. You could almost see your reflection in his shoes.

His appearance meant so much to him and he could never understand why I wouldn't wear a tie when I was on television. Indeed if he saw any of our well-known TV presenters without a tie on he'd give out yards and be hard pressed not to write in to RTÉ to complain!

Around about 2006 I began to notice the occasional change in my dad's appearance. He would turn up at a family function with a stain on his tie or he would wear a blue tie with a green jacket. I didn't pass many remarks at the time, but soon I became aware that he wasn't taking as much care about his appearance as he had always done. He also gave up fishing (his main passion) around then and went out walking less and less. By Christmas 2009 he wouldn't budge out at all and the cold winter of 2010 saw him go deeper and deeper into himself. In February that year he was admitted to hospital and became so remote from the world that I felt like shaking him back into life.

On 14 July 2010 Dad slipped away to wherever we go when we die. Right up to the last I thought he would come back to his old film-star self. Sadly it wasn't to be. I lost a true friend that day. He was someone I had seen almost every day of the previous thirty years and I miss our discussions and arguments, his silly jokes and most of all his appearance.

CHARLIE McGETTIGAN

## THE ROSE

I love going to the movies but I love it most of all
when it is in the company of my grandchildren. Last
year we saw many movies together and watching my
grandson Pádraig fall out of his seat laughing at the
various features we went to was just great fun. I
experienced 3D for the first time when we saw *Toy
Story 3*. This was supposed to be a treat for my
grandchildren but I think I had as much, if not more,
fun than they did! When I was a child they had what
they called 3D but it was a complete fraud. This
modern 3D really works and makes you want to reach
out to touch the characters or to duck when various
missiles are thrown from the screen in your direction.
It's fantastic. Not only were the special effects great,
but also the storyline, the characters and the voice-
overs by actors such as Tom Hanks as Woody and
Tim Allen as Buzz Lightyear were brilliant. The Toy
Story series of movies has been a phenomenal
success and I didn't think Pixar could top the first
two, but *Toy Story 3*, when Andy is leaving his toys
behind to go to college, had me and my grandchildren
laughing, crying, ducking and diving throughout –
definitely a highlight of the year.

## *Actor Eamon Morrissey*

Eamon Morrissey was born in Dublin and boasts a long and impressive theatrical career, most notably for the part of Ned, the emigrant, in the 1964 world première of Brian Friel's *Philadelphia, Here I Come!* He currently plays Cass Cassidy in RTÉ television's *Fair City*.

## THE ROSE

My rose and thorn may seem trivial compared with the massive problems faced by individuals and the nation last year, but they are nonetheless real to me. My rose is the double-sided, wood-burning stove we got installed during the summer in our L-shaped living room in Dublin. It now stands elegantly right at the heart of the house, its windows on two sides

spreading heat and warmth to both sections of the room and indeed throughout the house. There has been a dramatic drop in the use of oil in the central heating, as the output from the wood stove is four times that of a standard log fire.

I love trees, I love forests and I love logs. 'Bottled sunshine' is what I call logs. A log that I cut during the summer is placed in the stove and there is a great satisfaction in watching it light up and release its heat and sunshine into a winter's night. In my few acres in Wicklow, I have planted enough trees to absorb more carbon dioxide than I will ever produce, so I am not adding to the pollution problem. This is not a recent conversion to the environment; it is the achievement of a lifelong ambition.

The stove is not just a 'big boys' toy'. Ann has taken to it as well, and is as adept with it as myself. Tending and cleaning the stove is not just another chore, it is part of a lifestyle. During the winter of last year it was a great comfort to turn from the increasingly bleak news on the television to watch the dancing flames from the black stove reflecting on the white walls, and to have the security of knowing that there were more logs where the burning ones came from. Of course there is a slight thorn in the rose – isn't there always! The question is, at my age, for how

much longer will I be able for the chainsaw? But we will deal with that when the time comes.

## THE THORN

My thorn for last year has a connection with my rose, but as I say, there always is. Impassable roads prevented me from getting a load of logs out of Aughavannagh, so in the thaw after Christmas I went down to get them. As I drove into the little yard, I saw the cascade of water pumping out of the attic and down the wall of the house. That was on the outside. Inside was even worse. Talk about a water feature! I had to put on a raincoat to wade into the kitchen, where to my horror I saw the water pouring down over the press containing the fuse box, and the power was still on. This was dangerous.

I turned off the water supply and turned on the taps to empty the system. Don't ask me why I didn't turn off the water when I left before Christmas; it only makes me feel worse about the whole thing. The cascade reduced to a steady drip but most of it was coming down over the fuse box. The ESB had recently upgraded its supply point and there now seemed to be no way I could turn off the power.

Somewhat guiltily, I rang my neighbours. I always

seem to pester them when things go wrong. Their reaction was instant. In a couple of minutes John was on the doorstep to inspect the damage. Meanwhile his wife, Mollie, had located a local electrician and he was on his way. By the time the electrician arrived John was off searching for the burst pipes. The electrician quickly assured us that the system was safe, and then, since there was no work for an electrician, he turned plumber and fixed one of the leaks. That is the sort of people I am fortunate to have around me. That evening I was left with power, heat and a cold water supply. As if I wanted more of that stuff!

I began the awful clean-up, mopping up bucket after bucket of water from the downstairs floors; and cutting, pulling up and dumping yards of sodden carpet from the bedroom. It was awful. It is not as if it is a designer residence – it is largely furnished with forty years of 'hand-me-downs' – but still. At last, I crept into a dry corner and slept uneasily.

Overnight there was a new calf born. John took time to see all was well, and time to enjoy the spectacle of this new life exploring the world. As he says, 'Taking your time is the important thing.' And then this lifelong hill farmer insisted on turning plumber again. He had his 'bucket of bits' with him. He dismissed my idea of getting someone in, 'How would you get

a plumber up here during the holidays?' With skill, strength and most of all ingenuity from his 'bucket of bits', he repaired six leaking pipes and everything was working again. And then he was gone, as if he had simply stopped for a chat over the fence while he was feeding the cattle. As he says, 'Taking your time is the important thing.'

As I continued with the horrible clean-up, I began to see what had happened as a microcosm of what has happened to Ireland. What went wrong happened very quickly, and yet if I had paid more attention to regulation and control by turning off the water earlier, the damage would not have been as bad. Sound familiar? I was angry, frustrated, depressed and confused about what to do. Sound familiar? If I had called in the ESB and professional plumbers, I might still be waiting for power and water to be restored. My problem was solved by the kindness and ingenuity of the local people. And yes, the place is in a mess, but it was already in a decaying mess, and maybe this is an opportunity for a new beginning.

Over the years, John and I have occasionally sat before the log fire with a drop of whiskey and solved the problems of the nation. Or, we have at least solved them to our own satisfaction for that particular evening. But that is all on the theoretical side. In

reality, if my thorn was a microcosm of the nation's situation, then the way forward must surely be to accept what has happened, use the opportunity to find new and better ways, rely on our own local resources, and of course be blessed with neighbours like John and Mollie Keogh.

## *Sr Deirdre Mullan RSM*

Sr Deirdre Mullan is a Sister of Mercy from Derry, where she taught for two decades. She is currently Director of Mercy Global Concern at the United Nations, New York. 'As a teacher, I feel privileged to interact and work with young people. When asked what I do for a living, I usually reply, "I touch the future – I TEACH".' – Christa McAuliffe

THE THORN

Christina Taylor-Green was born on 11 September 2001. She was one of fifty babies born on that day, 9/11, which is remembered as one of the darkest days in human history. These births heralded hope at a time of despair. By all accounts Christina was a bubbly child and loved life. As she grew in awareness of the

significance of her birth-date, she began to take an interest in politics and in how our world operates. And so it was that she went with childlike enthusiasm to an open-air event in Tucson, Arizona, to meet her local representative. While there, Christina was gunned down by a young man, just thirteen years older than her.

What are we doing to our young people in this gun-crazed, spirit-crushing, fast-paced competitive society in which we live?

In any dark time, there is a tendency to veer towards thinking how much is wrong in our world. Do not focus on that. Focus on the children and stretch out and mend the part of the world within your reach. Let us build a world worthy of Christina's life.

THE ROSE

On 12 January 2010, for forty-five seconds, the land shook and Haiti was devastated. Over the following weeks and months heroic story after heroic story emerged from this island nation, which is a blight on the conscience of humanity. One such story that touched me deeply is that of a twelve-year-old boy called Pushon. He was one of the first children met by one of our sisters (a medical doctor) almost seventy-two hours

after the earthquake had devastated Haiti. His left leg was horribly crushed and was beginning to smell; it was obvious that the doctors would have to amputate or he would die. Pushon panicked when he heard this. 'No, no, no,' he begged, 'I can wiggle my toes.' When he was told that he would die if he did not have the amputation he became quiet and thought for a full minute. A minute is a long time in such circumstances.

Pushon wet his lips before he spoke. He had made up his mind. 'My father needs me,' he said. 'My mother is dead. My sisters are dead. My father needs me!' At the age of twelve, Pushon understood the implications of losing his limb in a country where poverty is especially harsh on the handicapped. He would never ride a bicycle again and gone were his dreams of becoming a doctor. Yet he chose to live, not for himself, but because his father needed him to live. He gave the most that he could give – his injured leg – so that his father might have strength and hope. 'What will my father do if I die?' he asked. Pushon had already seen the pain in his father's face after they lost his mother and sisters. The thought of his father losing everything was unbearable for the young boy. He decided to sacrifice his leg.

When you feel despair or a loss of hope, remember Pushon and reach out and help another.

## Don Mullan

Don Mullan, co-editor of this collection, is a native of Derry living in Dublin. He has campaigned on justice, peace and human rights issues throughout his life.

There are two roses and two thorns I wish to recall, one set is personal and the other global.

### THE PERSONAL THORN

It was Sunday, 20 March 2011, and I was returning to Rochester Airport in upstate New York to catch an evening flight to JFK, having spent the day visiting sites associated with Frederick Douglass, escaped slave and founder of the Civil Rights Movement of America. I had just paid the cab driver when my

mobile phone rang. 'Wendy Banks' appeared on the screen. Wendy is the eldest daughter of my boyhood hero, the great England goalkeeper, Gordon Banks. 'Don,' she said, 'have you heard about Terry Conroy?' Terry is a former Stoke City FC and Republic of Ireland soccer legend and a good friend of several years. I have often been a privileged guest at his home in Stoke-on-Trent. My mood rapidly changed from serenity to foreboding. I knew by the tone of Wendy's voice that there was something wrong. She told me that Terry had been rushed to hospital and was critically ill. My heart sank.

I immediately contacted another mutual friend, sculptor Andrew Edwards, whose friendship Terry introduced me to in 2006. Andrew hadn't heard but told me he'd find out and call me back. Ten minutes later he informed me that Terry had suffered a vascular aneurism and was in intensive care. The next twenty-four hours would be critical.

THE ROSE

My rose came a few days later when Andrew called to tell me that Terry had asked one of his daughters keeping vigil by his bedside, 'What was the score in the Chelsea and Manchester City game?' It was a

question from the mind of a man whose lifelong passion has been sport and a sign that his recovery is, thankfully, under way.

## THE GLOBAL THORN

Thérèse, our eldest daughter, called to me from downstairs to come and see the footage on Sky News of a major tsunami in Japan, following a 9.0 magnitude earthquake in the Tōhoku region. It was Monday, 11 March 2011.

The unpredictable and uncontrollable power of Mother Nature was shockingly captured by multiple eyewitness cameras. The entire world looked on helplessly as ships, trains, vehicles and entire villages were literally swept away like toys. It was traumatic to watch helicopter footage of cars and lorries being trapped as nearby highway ditches filled up and spilled onto roadways, engulfing unsuspecting drivers and their passengers. Some 28,000 people perished but one image that haunts me is of a solitary figure on a dirt track trying to outrun the black wave as it swallowed up the vegetation on either side of the field he or she was in.

My first thoughts were of a Japanese friend, Iku Kaneko, who is Japan's number-one U2 fan and who

has, for the past fifteen years, organised an annual fundraising event in Tokyo in support of the justice campaign of Derry's Bloody Sunday families and wounded. Her Irish friends were relieved when she made contact to say she was safe. On 30 March she emailed me: 'the earthquake was terrible . . . I was alone in the elevator because the company I work for is on the 30th floor of a very high building. I was alone and so scared to hear the automatic warning to get out! But I was trapped for several hours. We are still scared of aftershocks and radioactive contamination, but we have no choice but remain positive and smile . . . remembering there are situations worse in the world!'

As details of the disaster sunk in, memories began to surface of the January 2010 Haitian earthquake and of the December 2004 Indian Ocean tsunami. And while the death toll in Japan did not reach the level of those disasters, it was still shockingly high and the long-term consequences look ominous due to the damage inflicted on three nuclear power plants.

Memories of the March 1979 Three Mile Island nuclear crisis in Pennsylvania and the Chernobyl nuclear disaster of April 1986 surfaced. Through the heroic work of various Chernobyl charities, Irish people have witnessed first-hand the direct

consequences on children alive at the time and also the genetic damage inflicted on children born in the aftermath of that catastrophe.

In 1998 I interviewed the Nobel Laureate Archbishop Desmond Tutu, who said, 'We learn from history that we don't learn from history.' The tragic wisdom of this statement becomes clearer the older I get.

I had assumed that Japan would be nuclear free, given that it championed the banning of nuclear weapons following the atomic bombs that were dropped on Hiroshima and Nagasaki in August 1945. To learn that there are in fact fifty-five nuclear reactors in Japan, and that some of these were knowingly built on seismic fault lines is, pure and simple, insanity. Such a judgement is further supported by the discovery that expert warnings of potential disaster in the event of an earthquake were ignored by the Japanese Government.

It is to be hoped that Japan's nuclear crisis will be a wake-up call to governments around the world that risks, no matter how minimal the statistics might suggest, cannot be countenanced. We have no choice but to make cleaner sources of energy a global priority.

Sadly, following the earthquake and tsunami the added news of Japan's nuclear disaster has been a

multiplication of thorns that will likely mutate in unforeseen ways in years to come.

## THE ROSE

At Rochester Airport, before boarding my flight to JFK, I bought a copy of *Time* magazine with the cover headline 'Japan's Meltdown'. One comment made by a 24-year-old Japanese woman really caught me. It was weighed by the trauma just visited upon the nation and yet it was filled, like Iku's email above, with dignity, resilience, history and hope. 'We, the young generation, will unite and work hard to get over this tragedy,' Mamiko Shimizu said. 'It's now our time to rebuild Japan.'

It reminded me of the oft-quoted segment from the inaugural address of President John F. Kennedy on the steps of the US Capitol on 20 January 1961 and which is etched into granite at his gravesite in nearby Arlington National Cemetery: 'ask not what your country can do for you; ask what you can do for your country'.

Mamiko's comment was, for me, the first flowering of the rose: the determination of the younger generation to take responsibility for building a better Japan and, hopefully, a better world. I pray that

DON MULLAN

Mamiko Shimizu's generation do learn from history so that the lessons of 1945 and 2011 are not repeated, for the sake of future generations in Japan and across the globe.

## *Broadcaster Mike Murphy*

Mike Murphy is a former broadcaster with RTÉ and is a successful businessman. He is an Executive Director of Harcourt Developments, which has interests throughout Ireland, Britain, the Caribbean and the United States.

THE ROSE

My first grandchild, Mack, is eighteen months old. He has brought me joy that I wouldn't have believed was possible. I had often wondered what sort of a grandparent I'd be. I felt that I was a fairly good father, but wished that I had spent a bit more time with my children than I did. Mack gives me such pleasure and such joy. I love watching him grow. He now knows me and he seems to enjoy my company and I just

love the idea of him being there and being in my thoughts. Also, there is of course that wonderful liberty of being able to wave farewell and hand him back, of just doing the babysitting!

## THE THORN

I don't want to be clichéd but I would like to refer to an aspect of the economic and financial mess that we currently find ourselves in. Namely, the perennial greed and ostentaciousness of the senior banking people who awarded themselves huge salaries and bonuses and who have helped themselves to so much of what used to be *our* money. 'Official Bankdom Ireland Inc.' claimed that these people were irreplaceable and if they went on the job market they would be snapped up by other institutions and commercial companies, hence they had to be paid their gigantic salaries and bonuses. Now that most of these financial gurus are in the free market, by dint of either being fired or resigning, how many of them have been invited to join any independent company as a board member or as an adviser? Less than one per cent. They conned us as regards their own ability. I know from meeting so many of these people throughout my years at Harcourt Development that

they were simply a greedy mediocrity that helped themselves.

## *Senator David Norris*

David Norris was born in the Belgian Congo and has been in Seanad Éireann, as an independent senator, since 1987. In March 2011 he announced his intention to run as an independent candidate in the presidential election.

THE ROSE

The rose has been some wonderful evenings in Cyprus when I went swimming by moonlight from a deserted beach with an old friend. She is hopefully recovering from a serious illness and it was magical to float around in the warm water and discuss the meaning of life, politics, philosophy and religion.

DAVID NORRIS

## THE THORN

The thorn, of course, is the appalling economic situation. I am not sure if people realise that what we are witnessing is the greatest transfer of wealth from the poor to the rich that I have seen in my lifetime. I also get apoplectic with rage at the impertinence of the so-called ratings agencies – which got everything wrong and were seriously implicated in the toxic bundles stink that started the whole economic decline – in continuing to presume to give their so-called 'ratings' to the Irish economy.

## *Businessman Denis O'Brien*

Denis O'Brien is Chairman of the privately owned Digicel Group, one of the world's fastest-growing cellular companies. He also founded Communicorp Group, which owns and manages a portfolio of media-related companies in Ireland and seven other European countries.

## THE ROSE

The optimism I see in my children, in the questions they ask, in their belief that the problems of hunger and injustice in the world can, and will, be solved. The smiles on the faces of the children I see in places that have been ravaged by natural disasters or by appalling poverty and the hope in their eyes that somehow, someday, something will happen to make

their lives better. In Ireland, the determination of those who work towards bringing the country out of recession – from the individual who gets up every day to find employment to those running businesses.

## THE THORN

The obstacles that people put in the way of getting things done following calamities. The bureaucracy that gets in the way when efforts are being made to improve the lives of many with real benefit initiatives. It is so often back to the question of 'why?' rather than 'why not?' I think we can be, and must be, more optimistic in Ireland about the future. Our parents placed their hope in us. We should do the same with our children. Negativity simply does not get results.

## *Show Jumper Cian O'Connor*

Cian O'Connor is an Irish international show jumper at the highest level of the sport and has competed successfully all over Europe, the Middle East and the United States. He is currently ranked fifty-seventh in the world.

THE ROSE

I had a pretty good year. The rose would be finding my new horse K Club Lady and performing in Aachen in Germany, where we jumped a double clear round. We work tirelessly in this job to get a bit of success, so when you get it it's very enjoyable. In terms of Aachen, it's the world stage at the highest level you can get to and to go there with a horse that I got only three months beforehand and then to

jump two clear rounds was, I feel, a great achievement.

I always want to do well at the Dublin Horse Show and it was great when we got joint second place in the Aga Khan Trophy. My business is also going quite well. I'm involved in a lot of coaching, in jumping in the Middle East and in teaching out there, and in trying to organise to get people to come to Ireland and train.

## THE THORN

The low point would be that my other main horse suffered a knock. It is a pity when that happens, but I haven't got much to complain about really.

## *Author Joseph O'Connor*

Dublin native Joseph O'Connor is author of the novels *Cowboys and Indians*, *Desperadoes*, *The Salesman*, *Inishowen*, *Star of the Sea*, *Redemption Falls* and *Ghost Light*, as well as a number of bestselling works of non-fiction.

## THE ROSE

I am the most fortunate and blessed adult I know, and so I had roses a-plenty last year. The most beautiful bloom of all is the one to whom I have been married for twelve years, who is more lovely, more kind, more sexy, more smart, more giving, more forgiving, more humane, more compassionate, than anyone I have ever met in my life. We have two buds, aged six and ten, who often make me laugh till

it hurts. They are the sweetest and most intelligent and most warm-hearted boys in the world, and I consider myself honoured beyond belief to be their father.

What else? Well, Yeats said a man's greatest glory in life is his friends, and I hope to one day deserve the truly wonderful friends I have. With three of them – Philip King, Robbie Overson and Maureen Kennelly – I was involved in putting on a show of music and prose at the Peacock Theatre in Dublin in October. I got to read from my books, to share that noble stage with some of the greatest musicians in the country, and even to play guitar for such heroes of mine as Sinead O'Connor, Paul Brady and the band Scullion. I also had a novel published last year, *Ghost Light*, and its reception in Ireland truly touched my heart.

THE THORN

Thorns? Yes indeed. Did any of us not have some? There were big worries about the future and all the economic chaos, and a sadness at seeing my country get into the state it's in. I am not especially patriotic but I do feel an affinity with any Irish person, and it was shocking to see the sufferings being endured by

people, particularly as the year wore on and it became clear that things were going to get worse.

A friend of mine, Bernie, the wife of my dear friend Dermot Bolger, passed away suddenly in May. She was a truly lovely and special person and all of us miss her. Her death at such a young age put all the more passing problems of life into perspective, and the dignity and love of Dermot and their sons was so touching as to be heroic in my eyes.

## Former Minister Mary O'Rourke

A native of Athlone, County Westmeath, Mary O'Rourke is a former Fianna Fáil TD for the Longford–Westmeath constituency. She has previously served as Minister for Education, Minister for Health and Minister for Public Enterprise.

## THE THORN

This was my nephew Brian Lenihan's pancreatic cancer. I know many people and many loved ones are struck down with cancer all over the country, but the shock of hearing this news was immense. Brian had had a tummy ache that he could not identify and had been sent by his local doctor to the Mater Hospital for a scan. Very shortly after that we heard the dire

result. The force of it hit us just before Christmas, so for Brian's own family and then for the wider Lenihan family it was a Christmas that will never be forgotten. It was a double blow because in Brian we see all of the fine traits of his father, Brian, and his mother, Ann. In political terms his father will always be Camelot and with him gone young Brian (as we persist in calling him) had become the torch bearer for the family.

Christmas 2009 was miserable and as last year began the thorns struck deep and long. I thought a lot and cried a lot and I went back to my childhood prayer of the Memorare, which seems to give me great comfort when said aloud.

THE ROSE

On 27 January last year I got a rose in that my second son, Aengus, and his wife, Lisa, had their fourth child, a little baby boy. They christened him Scott and he is beautiful, but the really rosy part of it all is that I was invited to be his Godmother, the first time I was so invited out of six grandchildren. I love all six of them with a real strong physical love and now Scott is my crowning petal. He is a beautiful baby, all smiles, rolling around and attempting to sit up and then

stand up. Of course it helps that he has three young siblings – Luke, Sarah and James, all of whom love him and play with him and spend time with him so that he is raised in a home full of laughter, tears and deep, deep love.

Writing this makes me realise that even in the thorn of Brian's cancer there was a budding rose waiting to emerge. This was in the calm, rational way in which he dealt with his illness. He spoke about it and dealt with it in the privacy of his heart and his home but also softened to tell the country about it. So is there a lesson from the above stories? Yes, I think there is. Even the prickliest of thorns can have a rose underneath it and the rosiest of roses is about new life, new hope and new optimism.

## Goal's John O'Shea

John O'Shea founded aid agency GOAL in 1977 and is its Chief Executive. Since its inception, GOAL has spent more than €650 million on humanitarian programmes in almost fifty countries.

THE ROSE

The rose during last year was the time I got to spend with my family, particularly my grandchildren. It is never long enough, or often enough, so I cherish every minute. The joy of spending time with a grandchild is indescribable, so I won't try, but will make do with simply recommending it as the supreme form of blissful relaxation.

JOHN O'SHEA

## THE THORN

The thorns have been so many it would be impossible, indeed unfair in my line of work, to choose only one. I will settle for three particularly painful thorns: the Haiti earthquake in January that killed an estimated 270,000 people, injured another 300,000 and left 1.5 million homeless; the post-monsoon flooding in Pakistan, which swamped one-fifth of the country (an area the size of Italy), killed 1,600 people and left another eight million homeless; and the severe food shortages in Niger that had millions facing starvation.

After more than thirty years, I have become used to disasters, but I have never become hardened to them. If anything, as time goes by they affect me more. With so much heartbreaking first-hand experience, I know the realities behind the headlines. I know what survivors are going through, and what they will go through for years to come, long after the cameras and the reporters have gone and the world has lost interest. I suppose if I ever did become hardened to it, it would be time to quit. A constant frustration is the complete lack of preparation by the international community for these humanitarian catastrophes. We obviously can't predict precisely where or when they will strike, but we can be absolutely certain that periodically they *will*

strike. Yet, each time something happens it's as though it is the first time. It's like reinventing the wheel every time we have to make a journey.

## *Senator Feargal Quinn*

Feargal Quinn began his Superquinn business in 1960. He first ran for Seanad Éireann in 1993 and was re-elected in 1997, 2002 and 2007. In 2006 he was appointed an Adjunct Professor in Marketing at the National University of Ireland Galway.

### THE ROSE

My rose of last year was my new career as a television presenter in the RTÉ programme *Feargal Quinn's Retail Therapy*! It is a joy to have met a new challenge in the year that Superquinn celebrated its fiftieth birthday. However, the real rose is that I discovered there are people in the real world who are able to lift themselves out of a 'doom and gloom' economy and prove that they can succeed.

On the TV show, I visited six shops in different parts of Ireland – all of them in different businesses with different challenges facing them. We learned that, with a new pair of eyes looking at their situation, it was possible to overcome the feeling that nobody does well in tough times. Kim, the florist in Dublin's Liberties, grew in confidence in front of our eyes. Denis in Cobh began to 'wow' customers who had not visited his shop before. Florence in Claremorris set such a standard that her neighbouring shops also spruced up their offering. Rosie and her dad in Athlone proved that even the oldest department store in Ireland can set new standards. Fionnuala and Derek in Finglas were bright and optimistic after some original doubts. The optimism and creativity of the Savage family and their team in Swords was a real rose in spite of the thorn of losing JC himself the week before the programme was aired. So, six roses to prove that, even in difficult times, there is an air of 'can do' in Ireland – let's hope it will not only survive but also blossom in the years ahead.

## THE THORN

My thorn has been the loss of Rousseau, our great big family dog, who left this life in his twelfth year.

Rousseau was a big dog – a Briard who would frighten anyone who did not know him. A wonderful watchdog, I used to explain to people that as a sheepdog he would bite only on the inside of the thigh so the bite marks would not show! But Rousseau did not know he was a dog. At times when he would come over the Hill of Howth with us when we were on horseback, he thought he was a horse and kept up with us no matter how fast we galloped or how high we jumped. Rousseau loved children and they loved him. Our grandchildren learned to love animals from their experience with him and on one occasion his barking alerted us to a youngster wandering close to a cliff edge overlooking Jameson Beach on Howth Head. We will miss Rousseau and I find it difficult to believe that we will find another four-legged friend to take his place.

## *Arts Activist Pauline Ross*

Pauline Ross is one of the most influential arts activists in Northern Ireland. Born and raised in Derry, she is founder/director of the city's Playhouse Theatre, overseeing its award-winning renovation in 2009. It is now the largest community arts centre in Ireland, and one of the most artistically diverse.

## THE THORN

Early on the morning of 25 November I received the briefest of texts from my son John who works in Manchester in the construction industry. It read, 'Australia or New Zealand! Done!' My heart sank. The brevity of the text told me he had his mind made up. I was about to lose my son to a faraway country that can offer him work. In the early 1960s I

remember pleading with my father, who like thousands of other Derry men and boys never knew work, to take us all to Australia on the ten pounds passage. I was the eldest of eight children and even though only a young girl I was acutely aware of the social and political injustices practised in my city and was not hopeful for our future. Little did I know then that some fifty years later my own son would embark on the journey that I never got to take. Like thousands of other young Irish men and Irish women, all educated and highly skilled, he is now part of the twenty-first-century Irish exodus.

## THE ROSE

On the afternoon of 15 June last year, under a cloudless, bright blue sky, I like thousands of others walked in eager and nervous anticipation to the Bloody Sunday Memorial in Derry's Bogside. We gathered there before the march to Guildhall Square, where we would listen to and watch David Cameron's speech on the findings of the Saville Report into the killings of innocent marchers on Derry's Bloody Sunday Civil Rights March on 30 January 1972. What happened there in that square is now written into the annals of Derry's history. David Cameron's

speech was like a healing balm that cleansed our streets where blood had flowed and lives had been lost on that fateful Sunday. His words were sincere: 'on behalf of the government and indeed our country I am deeply sorry'. People wept tears of relief. We were all witnessing another 'Relief of Derry'. Everyone hugged and clapped and cheered and when the families of the dead emerged from inside the historic Guildhall the crowd spontaneously erupted in joy. It was the longest standing ovation I have ever experienced.

## *Former Minister Eamon Ryan*

Eamon Ryan was first elected to Dáil Éireann in 2002 for the Green Party. He was appointed Minister for Communications, Energy and Natural Resources in 2007, a post he held until January 2011. He lost his seat in the February 2011 general election.

THE ROSE

The relative warmth and sunshine of August in the west of Ireland was for me the rose of last year.

THE THORN

Anglo-Irish Bank has been a thorn in all our sides.

## *Author John Scally*

A native of Roscommon, John Scally is the author of more than twenty books. His forthcoming book is *100 Irish Rugby Greats*.

## THE THORN

My most enduring memories of my father are of horses on summer days. He would carry a bag with two bottles of tea wrapped in old stockings, a five-naggin whiskey bottle for him and a naggin bottle for me as we went off to save the hay. Just to be in his company made me feel that the world was in season. I loved going with him to the bog. Although it is backbreaking work, there is something special, almost spiritual, about the bog. The scent of turf fires and bog tea is a sensory pleasure. Although it is very exposed terrain when the weather turns nasty, when the sun was shining on me I always felt that God was smiling on the world. Everything was in harmony. It was my very own garden of Eden.

My happiness was not to last. On an October Saturday when I was five years old my father died. He was thirty-five. Looking back now I mourn for the unfinished business between us: so many things I would like to say but never got the chance.

THE ROSE

When my father died my grandfather became possibly the most important person in my life. I was called after him. Even his birthday was the same as mine. If there was one reason why I loved my grandfather so much it was that he always listened to me. He never cut me off in midstream. I always felt that he valued my opinion even when my ideas were totally harebrained. I was deeply grateful that he was living with us, otherwise I would have been a 'Mammy's boy' without a dominant male in my life. Although I was physically like my father, I inherited many of my grandfather's characteristics and qualities. The gap of a generation between us did not seem to matter.

Whenever it was necessary he had no hesitation in bringing me down a peg or two, but criticism was always tactfully offered. In the cosseted comfort of his presence I learned much about patience, kindness and selflessness.

In the softness of the western mist as I walk the fields of our family farm from which my heart can never be departed, I see his face. This land opens questions about my history and identity and goes further to some secret compass point that directs me to somewhere I do not know. In these fields people long dead live again, somehow speaking to years that belong to people not yet born. The ghost of my grandfather will always live in these fields, and in my heart.

## *Charity Director Kathi Scott*

Kathi Scott from Northern Ireland is Executive Director for the Nelson Mandela Children's Fund UK and Head of Europe for the Nelson Mandela Children's Hospital Capital Campaign. She was the first recipient of a Kids Taskforce Champion Award, recognising her outstanding achievements in protecting children.

## THE ROSE

I'd say that last year was filled with lots of little roses rather than a blooming great big one. The first little rose to appear was my gorgeous niece, Róisín, born in Dublin at the beginning of January. The first grandchild in our family, and naturally, not being biased at all, I'd have to say she is the most adorable little person all wrapped up in pink. One year on, she is a real live wire, spending her days running everywhere with a permanent smile. Our little rose brings so much love into our lives as a family. My next blossom came the following month when I was thrilled to meet Her Majesty Queen Elizabeth II at Buckingham Palace for the first time. The experience lived up to everything I had ever imagined it would be, and that's another item I've scored off my bucket list. The time I spend with my best friend, Michael, is very precious to me and during the summer we had the most wonderful evening at the open-air ZZ Top concert in Monaco, eating hot dogs with lots of old rockers and reliving our youth. My final rose of the year came in the form of a lovely big bunch from my boyfriend, Keith. We met days before my birthday in August, and having been single for so many years, what a lovely way to enter a new year, with someone special to share it with . . .

THE THORN

Having worked in the charity sector for many years, I've encountered people all over the world who face horrific challenges and obstacles. I love my job because it means I can play a very small part in helping people to improve the quality of their lives. The thorn of last year for me was the frustration of trying to fundraise for good causes in a financial downturn. We all know that charities are the first to suffer when people at home and in boardrooms are tightening their belts. But the impact is massive on those who need help the most, and particularly on children who are the most vulnerable in society. I felt the pressure, not only because the working hours got even longer and the pile of rejection letters grew more and more, but also because there are so many children out there who for the sake of a small amount of money wouldn't be hungry, but could be safe and warm, healthy and happy. That thorn often struck deep, keeping me awake at night and unfortunately still does . . .

## *Singer Eleanor Shanley*

Eleanor Shanley, from County Leitrim, has performed with De Danann, the late Ronnie Drew, Christy Moore, Sharon Shannon and many others. Her albums include *Eleanor Shanley*, *Desert Heart* and *A Place of My Own*.

THE ROSE

There were many roses for me during the last twelve months. It was a good year for me personally. Some of the highlights were reuniting with De Danann after many years and making the album *Wonderwaltz*. Performing with them at Skagen Festival, Denmark, the All Ireland Fleadh Ceol in Cavan and Campbells in Headford and, of course, my home gig in the Carrick-on-Shannon Water Music Festival was special.

Other highlights were touring with Sharon Shannon; most memorably, having the privilege of singing 'Fairytale of New York' with Shane McGowan; performing with Frankie Lane and Paul Kelly, our most enjoyable gigs of the year being the National Concert Hall (Concertgebouw) in Amsterdam, Ionad Dara in Goresbridge and Caherciveen Festival (with Mike Hanrahan); and being part of the 'Folk the Recession' gigs in Walkinstown! The year ended off on a very nice note when I recorded 'My Angel' with Patrick Bergin. A song written by Patrick and based on the African song 'Malaika' (Angel).

For many years now my visits to Inisbofin Island off the Galway coast have been the highlight of my year and last year was no different. Inisbofin is my haven away from home and I visit there at every given opportunity. I am lucky to have a hugely supportive family and great friends and last year was kind to all of us so I can ask for no more in that respect.

## THE THORN

I lived through 1970s and 1980s Ireland and watched my friends and family members emigrate in search of work and a better life. During the 1990s this changed and rural Ireland became vibrant and for the

first time since the Famine the population of my home county, Leitrim, increased. It was a joy to socialise and witness the prosperity of the locality and the healthy increase of the young population. My thorn is my sadness at seeing all this taken away by the greedy, irresponsible few who recklessly destroyed all that was good. The increase in emigration and the surge in 'going away' parties for people once again taking that uncertain road to Britain, the United States, Canada or Australia are frightening and disheartening. I can only hope that there will be a turnaround soon and Ireland will be that land of opportunity for future generations if they choose to stay here.

## Singer Rebecca Storm

Rebecca Storm has always loved to sing and successfully auditioned for her first musical part in *Blood Brothers* at just twenty-three years of age. In 2000 she released *I Want to Know What Love Is* and in 2003 *Celtic 'n' Broadway*, recorded with sixty wonderful musicians.

## THE THORN

It took me longer than most to get 'into' this computer 'techknowledgy'. In fact my daughter and nephew had mobile phones way before me. However, a few years ago my husband, Kenny, insisted he organise a website for me. I laughed, but of course now I can't imagine life without it. Last year it brought me the rose and the thorn at the same time.

I loved my schooldays and my dear friends Lesley, Kim and Barbara. Nevertheless, when I got the opportunity to leave the small town of my birth and head down to London for the lights of the West End, I was off in a shot. So much happened so fast, with many new and exciting friends to spend all my time with. We four had all gone on to different colleges or universities and sadly I lost touch with them for over thirty years. Until last year, when I received an email via my website from Lesley. I was so excited as I read her first couple of paragraphs. The 'three musgirltears' had managed to get back in contact and met up from time to time. They had chatted about getting in touch with me. With a marriage and a 'showbiz' change of name, I obviously hadn't made it easy and thought they had just forgotten me. However, the email told me they had in fact been to see me in many shows, but were too embarrassed to get in touch. I was almost cross, but forgave them as I was so happy to hear from them. That is until I read on and discovered that the beautiful Barbara, who had been fitter than all of us and was a mother of two strapping sons, had died within forty-eight hours of catching swine flu. No one could believe it. What was it about this horrendous disease? That, of course, was the thorn.

## THE ROSE

The rose was that the three of us have since met up over dinner several times and can be again the great friends that we once were. Lesley's three children are all in the army out in Iraq and Afghanistan and Kim's beloved father has Alzheimer's. I too, although very happy, have had my share of sadness, so we now chat endlessly on the phone or email and cheer each other up. In fact with Kim's 'techknowledgy' we can have a three-way chat. One in Yorkshire, one in Wales and me here in Ireland! How clever is that? We always end up giggling our heads off and send love to Barbara for bringing us back together again. When I put down the phone, I thank the dreaded gadgets that I once shunned. Friends and family are everything and I'm so glad we can keep in touch.

Any more old pals out there, I'm at www.RebeccaStorm.com! Thanks Kenny, xx.

## Horse Trainer Ted Walsh

Ted Walsh is from Cork and one of his more famous achievements was training Papillon to win the 2000 English Grand National and Commanche Court to win the 2000 Irish Grand National, both ridden by his son Ruby. Ted's daughter Katie is also a jockey.

## THE ROSE

Being a racing family, my rose was seeing my youngest daughter, twenty-five-year-old Katie, ride her first winner, Poker de Sivola, on 17 March last year at Cheltenham. To witness her doing that and to see the joy in her face afterwards, and what it meant to her, was just fabulous. It was a great family occasion.

TED WALSH

## THE THORN

A very good friend of mine is very sick. I hope he pulls through and makes a good recovery. I'm a big man on health and happiness and my children and grandchildren mean a lot to me.

## *Painter Gary White Deer*

Gary White Deer is a Choctaw from Oklahoma who has been visiting Ireland regularly since 1994. He was commissioned by the Irish Government in 1997 to paint a representation of the Choctaw-Irish famine donation of 1847. He donated his US$20,000 fee to the Irish humanitarian agency Concern Worldwide.

### THE ROSE

The year before last I looked down on a hospital bed and watched my daughter tenderly hold a baby girl sent without life, Jincee tracing the lines of a tiny mouth that would never smile, a beautiful child who couldn't stay. Then Jincee carried another child, and we all waited and prayed. Now there is amazing

Desiree, my eighth grandchild, a baby with a wondrous smile, filled with life and who is blossoming as lovely as any rose. Little Desiree is powerful; she has lifted all our hearts.

My son Jesse is living on the sofa, my parlour looking like an older teenager's room. Of my seven children, Jesse was always the one who wanted to go places with me, the second youngest who loved being with his nieces and nephews. Then Jesse grew up, left his mother's house, struggled with bills and caught a little trouble: getting into car wrecks, losing a job for being hung-over. Last year I invited him to move in for a while. He was hesitant; he liked his freedom and probably thought I'd treat him like a valet or a seven-year-old. Now he's working steady and attending college. He goes as he pleases and always returns clear-headed. Jesse is special, although not special enough to drive my car just yet. But it feels good to have him around again.

Dun Laoghaire filmmaker Peter McCarthy organised a lecture tour with the Irish consulates of Chicago, New York and Boston, and I went along. We attended official events and it was very much an honour to meet President Mary McAleese. I had the chance to speak on the Choctaw donation to Famine Ireland and there was lots of fancy running toward

planes, trains, taxis and subways, with some good restaurants in between. Peter was great to hang out with and it's always fun to go and see.

## THE THORN

Last year I divorced. Standing outside tribal court, realising it was over, was difficult, and at times it still is. None of us marry expecting it to end; but sometimes not all of it does. On the anniversary of the divorce, my ex invited me for dinner, a quiet friendship that lingers. And the girl can still cook.

And a writer from Dublin did a story on me that hit most of the major US papers before it went global. Incredibly, the article claimed I discovered my tribal identity in Ireland after a scouring search. That didn't play well in Indian Country. A Zuni friend said the piece made me seem 'new-agey' and a Choctaw woman spammed the article with the header 'Lost Choctaw Found in Ireland', gleefully adding that I was a 'hattak tasembo', a crazy man. I've always denied being crazy, however.

This thorn may have a rose attached. I'd been busy avoiding a request for a memoir; now I'm busy writing one so I can tell my own story. Roses and thorns . . . we all have such stories.

## *Conclusion*

We hope you have enjoyed reading about the ups and downs in the lives of the contributors to this book and that it will persuade you to share your own roses and thorns with us for the next collection, details of which are given below.

What struck us most about the familiar names who contributed to this book were the positives outweighing the negatives. People spoke of their thorns – family illnesses, hardships, the economic climate, yet after they had written so vividly about the cruelness of life they chose to write about the resurrection of the image of the blooming rose: vibrant, beautiful and so real you can almost touch it. Their personal and striking stories conjure up strong and inspiring images of hope and richness. Every

person in this collection spoke of events and people and days when they had felt happy and loved or had perhaps brought a little sunshine into the lives of others.

Over fifty very diverse and individual people chose to contribute to this book and many memorable quotes come to mind as I reflect on the process of publication. Much-loved veteran actor David Kelly's words flowed strikingly, as he described the many blessings in his life, from his esteemed theatrical career to his cherished wife and his beloved dog: 'it doesn't have to be the rose season for me to enjoy rose after rose after rose,' he penned with deep emotion.

Fresh from the wave of grief that followed the death of Gerry Ryan, many of his RTÉ colleagues chose this compilation as a way to remember him, identifying his passing as the thorn in their lives from last year. John Creedon described him as 'one of our greatest broadcasters' and noted that his death 'wasn't in the script at all'. He contrasted Gerry's passing with the birth of his granddaughter, Mollie, his chosen rose, who was all the more precious because he had lost his first grandchild, Lucy. He concludes that 'death is not the opposite to life, death is the opposite to death and whatever energy keeps going round and round, that energy is universal and applies to those who went before us and those who will come after us'.

Politician Mary O'Rourke chose her nephew Brian Lenihan's very public battle with cancer as her thorn. Describing him affectionately as 'the torch bearer of the family', she recalls the Christmas that the news was so cruelly broken as a dark and depressing time but notes that Brian has shown great courage in his battle; one he appears to be winning. 'I thought a lot and cried a lot and I went back to my childhood prayer of the Memorare, which seems to give me great comfort when said aloud,' she wrote of that harrowing time. Choosing her grandchild Scott, her first Godson, as her rose and 'crowning petal', she said there was a lesson to be learned in the circle of life: 'Even the prickliest of thorns can have a rose underneath it and the rosiest of roses is about new life, new hope and new optimism.'

Former Eurovision winner and singer-songwriter Charlie McGettigan painted a poignant picture of a grown man, a son still grieving for a parent, as he described the sad decline of his father, whom he had recently lost. A 'handsome man' known for being 'really well turned out', Charlie tells us, began to 'turn up at a family function with a stain on his tie or he would wear a blue tie with a green jacket'. As time went on he deteriorated deeper into himself and was admitted to hospital. He 'became so remote from the world that I felt like shaking him back into life'. Eventually, 'Dad slipped away to wherever we go when we die. Right up to the last I thought he would come back to his old film-star self. Sadly it wasn't to be. I lost a true friend that day.'

The thorns in this book were often painful and raw but the roses were real and blooming, as evidenced by priest and singer Liam Lawton, who spoke lovingly of his once seriously ill eight-year-old nephew who had endured seventeen surgeries in his childhood. He recalled visiting the boy one night in hospital and witnessing a young Filipino nurse singing a beautiful lullaby to him. He wondered if the little boy would ever speak or sing himself, having undergone a tracheotomy.

But every day small blessings become great ones. Every act of kindness, no matter how small, becomes an opportunity for hope and healing. In this place of great vulnerability, the light of each new day makes room for miracles. The many days and nights have grown into years and the tiny little boy has grown to take his place in our world. Last year he stood before his community to read at the local vigil Mass. He spoke loud and clear and prayed for those less fortunate. His family rejoiced in this miracle. His name is Daniel: the one who enters the lion's den and is unharmed.

Finally, and perhaps most poignantly, Brian Carthy, sports commentator with RTÉ, captured the mood of the country following the tragic passing of Michaela McAreavey. He had attended her wedding and then her funeral a mere three weeks later. 'Thursday 30 December 2010,' he wrote, 'is a date etched in my mind. On that joyous day, in the tranquil setting of St Malachy's Church, Ballymacilroy in County Tyrone, the stunningly beautiful and radiant Michaela, with her husband John McAreavey by her side, told me it was the "happiest, happiest" day of her life.' He remembers how 'Michaela was so full of joy. She could not stop smiling.' Then he recalls 'the sense of shock and utter disbelief' when eleven days later 'Michaela was taken from us in devastatingly cruel circumstances'. He finishes with the observation that 'Truly, God was at his brilliant best the day Michaela was born.'

We would like to thank everyone who shared

## CONCLUSION

their roses and thorns with us for this publication in aid of the Irish Epilepsy Association and we invite you to unite with them to téll us your story for our next collection, which we intend to publish in late 2012. Please send us details of your rose and thorn for this new collection, which will reflect back on 2011 and 2012. You may email your stories, on any subject, in confidence to:
**myroseandthorn@gmail.com.**

**Audrey Healy**
**April 2011**

## *The Rose and the Thorn: An Allegory*

This past year, 2010, a transplanted hybrid tea rose bloomed in October in Dublin. Although in appearance she looks like a common rose in an Irish garden, when you hear her story your heart will see differently.

Five years earlier, in New Orleans, a rosehip had been severed from her stem by flying debris in winds of over a hundred miles per hour. The force of the winds slammed her against a concrete wall, splitting her open and spilling her microscopic seeds into rising floodwater.

When the floodwater receded over two months later, leaving a trail of mucky debris and toxic detritus, a tiny seed, exhausted from her lengthy travels, bedded down in an eerily silent neighbourhood that had been vacated by its frightened inhabitants at the height of Hurricane Katrina.

Tentatively, the seed put down her roots in this new wilderness, drawing enough sustenance to form a tiny shoot that grew into two soft, round green leaves. But the little rose plant knew she needed protection if she was to live in that desolate, deserted city. After months of hesitancy, she made up her mind to stay and pushed up a strong stem with a sharp, prickly thorn. One, two, three, four, five more thorns grew on that tall, straight stalk.

The thorns instinctively knew that they were her protectors but it was only when a soft swelling formed on the top of their stem that they realised the importance of their job. A delicate bud had formed! Keeping her green coat wrapped tightly around her body, the little bud grew daily under the watchful eyes of these armed guards.

However, the day came when not even the thorns could protect her from being uprooted and transplanted thousands of miles away to a country where the grass is emerald green and the rain falls often from the sky. Although the people of that country were kind and fed her well, the little bud shuddered for a long time and drooped her head on her tall stem.

# THE ROSE AND THE THORN: AN ALLEGORY

She even hesitated to put down her roots, causing her guards, the thorns, to whisper their concerns to each other. 'She's not thriving here.' 'I can't smell her sweet fragrance.' 'She's hiding her beauty.'

A senior thorn, closest to the little bud, confided to the others that he had peeped under her slightly open coat one day and observed that her skin was quite dark and even wrinkled. She was definitely ill!

'Let us get strong and brave and tell her that we'll protect her with our lives,' the senior thorn exhorted the other thorns. These words helped them to sharpen their points and stiffen in their resolve to protect the precious bud.

When she heard the thorns' pledge of loyalty, the little bud began to trust again and her confidence grew significantly. In a short time, she felt well enough to open her green coat for the pale sun to heal her body. But it was only when the people asked her to share with them her story, and she enthusiastically acquiesced to their request, that the thorns noticed that she had indeed become a confident young rose.

Young and old people began to come from far and near to hear her tell about her experiences when Hurricane Katrina's winds buffeted a proud American city and emptied millions of gallons of putrid water into its neighbourhoods. She could feel their hearts beating with hers and knew from the sadness in their eyes that they shared some of the pain she experienced.

The transplanted hybrid tea rose now feels that she belongs where the grass is emerald green. She tells her story to whomever shows interest and displays her array of finely shaped petals as she talks. She is now a sophisticated, crimson red beauty who wafts her sweet fragrance over her friends.

When she looks at the thorns, her thoughts often return to the place that was once called 'the City that Care Forgot' and to the many wonderful people who suffered so much in a terrible hurricane. But when the nametag in the middle of her stem, in a rose bed in an ordinary Irish garden, catches her eye, she smiles. What could be a better name for a red rose than Lasting Love?

**Maeve McMahon OP**

## Acknowledgements

Our first thank you must be extended to America's first family, the Obamas, whose dinner-time tradition of reviewing their day with the 'rose and thorn' game was the seed inspiration for this book. We also thank the journalists who first reported the story, ABC's Charlie Gibson and George Stephanopoulos, and the eminent Barbara Walters on ABC's *The View* for asking the question of President Obama. And a very big thank you to our own Aine Lawlor of RTÉ 1's *Morning Ireland* for her role in inspiring this book.

We are very grateful to all those who responded to our, perhaps unusual, request for contributions, some as far back as August last year. We thank you most sincerely for sharing the ups and downs in your life with such enthusiasm and honesty, particularly as

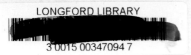
royalties for this publication will benefit a very worthy charity, Brainwave – the Irish Epilepsy Association.

Friends and family have also helped us enormously on this journey and we would like to thank them for their opinions and viewpoints, particularly Audrey's parents and her siblings, Thomas, Paul, Liam and Mark, and friends Fionnula, Deirdre V, Mary R, Kitty, Hilary, Sharon and all the gang, as well as Don's family, Margaret, Thérèse, Carl and Emma.

Special thanks to Charlie McGettigan and David Norris for reading early drafts and for agreeing to launch the book. Thanks to Mike Glynn, CEO of Brainwave, for his encouragement and support and for kindly hosting the Dublin launch and to county librarian Mary Carleton Reynolds and all the staff of Longford Library for hosting the Longford launch.

We also thank Don's publishing mentor, Seamus Cashman, editor Jennifer Armstrong, designer and artworker Glen Powell, and Ray Lynn of Beta Print Services.

Once again we thank the contributors and hope their submissions will encourage readers to search inside themselves and discover their own 'rose' and 'thorn'. We would be delighted to consider those for inclusion in our next edition.